POWER

★★★

Real Estate

★★★

ADVERTISING

★★★★★★★★★★★

The Complete Guide for Professionals

William H. Pivar
Bradley A. Pivar

Real Estate
Education Company
a division of Dearborn Financial Publishing, Inc.

Publisher: Kathleen A. Welton
Acquisitions Editor: Patrick J. Hogan
Associate Editor: Karen A. Christensen
Senior Project Editor: Jack L. Kiburz
Interior Design: Lucy Jenkins

Published by Real Estate Education Company,
a division of Dearborn Financial Publishing, Inc.

Library of Congress Cataloging-in-Publication Data

Pivar, William H.
    Power real estate advertising / William H. Pivar, Bradley A. Pivar.
        p.   cm.
    Includes index.
    ISBN 0-79310-158-1
    1. Advertising—Real estate business.   I. Pivar, Bradley A.
II. Title.
HF6161.R3P585   1991
659.1′933333—dc20   91–24520
                                      CIP

"Doing business without advertising is like winking at a girl in the dark. You know what you are doing, but nobody else does."

—Stuart Henderson Britt

Contents

Preface

The origin of the word *advertising* is the Latin *ad vertere*, which means "to turn the mind toward." After more than 2,000 years the purpose of advertising still is to turn the mind toward, in this case, the minds of others toward your product or service.

Good real estate advertising actually serves a number of purposes, including

- building a firm's image,
- building staff morale,
- keeping sellers happy,
- obtaining new listings,
- recruiting new salespeople and
- locating prospective buyers.

Advertising gives you the opportunity to sell yourself, your services and your products. However, no matter how good, your advertising alone doesn't sell real estate. Only people can sell real estate.

And even with good salespeople and good advertising, you will not realize sales without competitively priced products that meet the needs of buyers. Advertising is simply one element needed for success; however, without quality advertising you will have few opportunities to be successful. For example, one of the best advertising campaigns in recent history failed to turn the Isuzu into a top-selling vehicle, even though the public loved the ads.

It is not often that a real estate agent has input into the planning and building of a product to help the builder maximize its salability. The norm in real estate is to market the product as it is presented to us with all its faults and virtues. This even extends to exclusive listings. We don't control the product—not even its packaging. However, we can encourage owners to make their properties as attractive as possible for sales purposes. For suggestions on increasing the salability of homes through cleaning, painting, landscaping, etc., we strongly suggest you refer to the book, *Power Real Estate Listing* (Real Estate Education Company).

While cute and funny advertisements are pleasing, the purpose is not just to entertain. A good ad must do more than give information and create interest. An ad fails if it hasn't resulted in action. A good ad brings action, while a great ad not only results in action but also is remembered long after it has been used. In real estate, we want immediate action as well as the residual benefits of awareness and image. "Action" in real estate advertising is normally a telephone call, but it could also be a personal visit to your office, property or development.

Advertising should be, very simply, *truth well told.* Although advertising must be truthful, it must also have appeal to the extent that the recipient wants to know more. The best advertising can't improve your product, but it can improve a potential buyer's perception of that product. Ads can create an image of desirability and value, turning what was originally perceived by a buyer as a "want" into a "need." As an example, you can create a demand for second homes by making them appear to be more of a life-style necessity than a luxury. A good ad promotes what the reader or listener desires.

You probably have heard the adage, "Man would still be living in caves if it were not for the first real estate salesperson." Although it sounds a little facetious, there's more truth to this expression than jest.

There is a deep-seated idea that real estate is the road to wealth. While the 11th Commandment is not "Real estate always increases in value," real estate *is* responsible for more millionaires than any other source. Very few buyers will resent the fact they purchased real estate from you, and most will be eternally grateful. Promoting your products is a service to others, and not a foisting of a product on unwilling customers.

To begin with, you have a willing buyer. People want to become homeowners. They welcome ownership from the simple desire to live in their own home as well as for investment motives. Ownership to first-time owners provides a strong sense of security and control of their destinies. In addition to first-time buyers, you have previous homeowners who know the benefits of ownership. These buyers have strong aspirations to move up to homes better suited to their current needs and desires.

Power advertising is the use of all available media to maximize your results. Since most real estate advertising is aimed at prospective buyers, sellers, lessors and lessees, the results of power advertising would be reflected in optimizing the qualified buyer, seller, lessor and lessee contacts produced. Unqualified buyer, seller, lessor or lessee contacts produced through advertising are worse than no contacts at all. Such contacts serve to monopolize your time, becoming economic burdens rather than benefits. It is essential for your advertising to bring in contacts with the products and motivation to sell or lease, or the desire and ability to buy or lease property that meets their needs.

Although power advertising provides you with additional contacts to increase the effectiveness of your office, power advertising does not sell. It merely gives you an opportunity to meet the needs of your contacts. Many seminars and books explain what to do after you have made the contact. This book shows you how to obtain the positive response that leads to sales. The actual sales are up to you.

In this book we will be exploring more than just the usual classified ads. We will cover window displays, signs, billboards, property briefs, radio, television, direct mail and a great deal more. You will learn how to evaluate the cost-effectiveness of advertising and media, and how to develop and use a power plan for your office. Don't think of the many innovative ideas as mandatory rules, because the *first* axiom of advertising is there are no mandates. The unconventional can, and does, succeed.

1 Your Advertising Plan

Advertising is far too costly and important to leave to intuition or to waste by playing "follow the leader," copying what your competitors are doing. You must set a goal, devise a plan to meet that goal and then implement that plan.

WHY ADVERTISE?

In real estate advertising, you are selling two distinct products: the property advertised and your firm. Ads that only promote the property fail to fully utilize the ad's potential to create goodwill and prominent name identification in the market area. Name identification is important if you want to be in business through the next economic cycle. Firms that fail to develop a strong name presence in a market are those least likely to survive an economic downturn.

Institutional advertising sells your firm instead of the product. It can help you build long-term name recognition for your firm, but if you place too great an emphasis on it, your firm might not survive to enjoy the future. The best institutional advertising is actual success, as evident in a preponderance of For Sale and Sold signs which indicate a major marketplace presence.

The reason goodwill is so important in real estate can be summed up in one word: mobility. A survey by the Newspaper Advertising Bureau indicated that 25 percent of recent homebuyers expect to move again within the next four years, 40 percent expect to stay between five and ten years and the remaining 35 percent expect to remain more than ten years.

Local real estate activity is tied to the local economy, and success demands that your advertising budget be adjusted as the economy changes. However, an advertising plan must include a plan to establish or maintain your firm's market presence. If you are in a seasonal area, the season, like the economy, will dictate adjustments in advertising planning.

BUDGETING

Advertising budgets should be based on a percentage of projected office commission instead of historical figures, which could result in too great or too low an advertising budget. Many firms budget based on a percentage of *total* commission. This is an unrealistic figure to use; only those dollars that reach the broker are important. Some firms use the old rule of thumb that advertising should be 1 percent of gross sales. While it usually works out to be at about 30 percent of company dollars, this formula leaves no room for adjustment to conditions.

Because much of the broker's other overhead is fixed, the broker cannot apply the same percentage when volume decreases or the broker might be planning deficit spending. Accounting for these fixed costs, you should budget more for advertising in a time of high volume and less in periods when volume is anticipated to decline. For example, a firm that anticipates $300,000 in the company share of commissions might allocate 30 percent of these company dollars, or $90,000, for advertising. If, however, the economy changed and the firm expected only $150,000 in anticipated commissions as the company share, the broker might only allocate 20 percent of the commission money toward advertising or $30,000.

A new firm must establish a market presence, and would therefore use a higher percentage of anticipated office commission for advertising than would an established firm. If offset by an equal increase in office revenue, an increase in advertising would likely be a wise choice for a new firm even though it failed to increase profit.

It is possible, but unusual, for an office to buck an economic trend and successfully increase the advertising budget during a local recession. This does not, however, increase the percentage of commission spent on advertising. Brokers who can buck economic trends are basing their advertising budgets on an anticipated increase in volume, which they then work to obtain. These brokers are "contrarians." Successful contrarians are either doing the same as others, only better, or are doing something entirely different.

Advertising salespeople will tell you the time to expand your advertising is when everyone else is restricting their ads. In such a period it takes far fewer advertising dollars to be a major presence in the marketplace. Despite the exceptions, you generally can't buck a recession with increases in advertising. There is a point of diminishing returns where additional advertising dollars will not bring in revenues sufficient to cover the additional advertising costs.

The percentage of anticipated office revenues that should be allocated for advertising also varies by the marketplace. In smaller communities, where effective low-cost advertising is possible or where a greater percentage of sales is the result of personal relationships, a lower percentage might be possible. The percentage for that market might be inadequate to generate anticipated volume in a large metropolitan market where advertising costs are likely to be high. For example, a six-line classified ad, run for one month in the *Los Angeles Times* would cost more than $1,000. In some smaller market areas, the same size ad in a daily paper might run less than $100 for one month.

The type of property you sell will also affect your advertising budget. Some firms have achieved a predominant niche market in lots. Most of their listings are obtained by calling and visiting owners and most of their sales are to builders with whom they have worked for years. These firms also have a very low advertising budget.

In a seller's market where you can sell anything you can list, you should decrease the portion of your advertising dollar spent on sales and increase the percentage spent on securing more inventory.

You can never spend enough money on advertising to please all of your sales staff. Your salespeople would like to see you spend 110 percent of your office commission on advertising. Advertising brings in leads. While not the only source of leads, advertising leads come in without any effort by the salesperson. If you place ads to please salespeople, you will not be in business very long.

In the same vein, don't place ads to please owners. Owners would like to see half-hour television specials on their property coupled with double-page, full-color spreads in local papers. The purpose of advertising is to bring in qualified contacts your sales staff can then convert to completed transactions, not to keep people happy. Also, if you don't control a property, don't advertise it. Advertising open listings or verbal understandings is a formula for failure.

Advertising should not be regarded as just an expense; it is an investment in future income and, if well invested, will yield dividends. However, if invested without planning, your money will either fail to bring a return or will bring an inadequate return.

PLANNING

In planning your advertising you must consider media to be used and media cost. Changes in costs of a particular medium could affect the ways you allocate your advertising dollars.

Medium selection should be based on the medium's historical success, as determined through a cost-benefit analysis. Besides being effective in bringing in prospective buyers, the medium must also be cost effective based on the cost per prospect.

Test an advertising medium to determine the cost per contact. A lower cost per contact would likely mean greater emphasis on that medium. But just because you get poorer results from one medium does not mean you should abandon that medium. Ask if your firm could have reached the buyers through other, less costly advertising. Also ask if the buyers contributed to the overall profitability of the firm. In other words, the medium is still cost effective if the ad costs are more than offset by increased office revenue.

In your media selection consider where your buyers are coming from. Nationally, according to the Newspaper Advertising Bureau, two-thirds of buyers move less than 20 miles, which points out the importance of locally oriented media. The distance homebuyers move increases with both age and income, so for retirement housing and prestigious housing, your buyers are likely to come from a wider market area. Media selection is so important that advertising agencies use media directors who make media-use choices with the purpose of optimizing the net effect of advertising dollars.

Newspapers have "open rates" whereby the rate decreases with the greater use of space. Contract rates are significantly lower than open rates, but you must guarantee a total amount of space per billing period and often per issue. The more space you agree to use, the lower your overall rate will be. For example, one real estate firm acts as sales agent for several developments and places all their ads. The developers reimburse the firm for the ad costs. Because of the combined space contracted for by her firm, the real estate firm is able to obtain a very low advertising rate. The developer's clients also benefit by the lower combined rates. The underlying danger in this tactic is that bankruptcy of one or more of the developers could leave the firm personally liable for many thousands of dollars in advertising costs.

A major problem with contracts is the longer the term of the contract, the lower the rate. In striving to cut costs, many brokers sign long-term commitments for space. A downturn in the economy could leave a broker with overhead that exceeds income. Long-term contracts are risky in a cyclical business such as real estate.

Newspapers also give lower rates when the same ad is repeated. This can create a false economy, as ads repeated over a long period of time lose effectiveness. Readers look for new ads. If a property has been in the paper for a long time, readers might think something is wrong with it. We recommend an ad be repeated in no more than three consecutive editions of a daily or weekly paper. After that, if the broker wishes to continue to advertise the property, he or she should use another ad, possibly targeting a different appeal. This approach will have the same effect as a new ad on a new listing. An ad can be used again after three insertions; for a daily paper, however, wait at least three weeks. For a weekly paper, wait three weeks and then insert for one week only.

In your advertising planning, remember that people normally buy a different home than the one about which they first inquired. Therefore, a wide range of properties can be covered by advertising just a handful of them in various price ranges. After qualifying, prospects are of course shown several properties that meet their needs. If you follow this philosophy, make certain the owners understand that advertising similar properties in the same price range can bring in buyers for their homes as well.

In selecting properties to advertise, emphasize probabilities, not just possibilities. If the property's price is above market and the seller is not motivated, a sale would be a possibility, not a probability. Either get the price adjusted or return the listing. Advertising such a property would be a formula for failure. Brokers who advertise the possibilities generally end up acting as salespersons for wiser brokers.

In your advertising planning, consider the best time to advertise. Besides seasonal adjustments, weekends bring the most activity. For evening papers, Friday and Saturday should receive the greatest emphasis. If there is a Sunday morning edition, then you would not advertise in the Saturday evening newspaper. For morning papers, Saturday and Sunday editions should carry the bulk of your weekly ads.

A great many house hunters keep the Sunday home ads and inquire about them during the week. Higher income buyers tend to look for homes on weekends, while lower income home seekers are more likely to shop during the week. A recent survey by the Newspaper Advertising Bureau indicates that 36 percent of single buyers shop for homes only on Sunday.

Once an offer is accepted or an agency expires you must cease your advertising. You must have a system to indicate which properties are being advertised to cancel or modify ads. Real estate brokers throw away millions of dollars each year because they fail to cancel ads.

MEDIA SELECTION

There are many advertising media to choose from when marketing property. Although you will ordinarily be using more than one, there are times when you will only want to use a single advertising medium for a property. Using a single medium in promoting a particular property can offer you a great opportunity to monitor your advertising success: Simply keep track of all the responses to that ad to assess its cost-effectiveness.

You want your ad coverage targeted to the largest possible group of likely buyers.

A newspaper emphasizing the sensational might have a less educated and lower income readership than would a conservative newspaper. You also might find that the demographics from a very liberal newspaper indicate a young readership with a high percentage of college graduates.

To the greatest possible extent, you also want to avoid buying wasteful advertising. There will always be some waste coverage, as your market area will not coincide precisely with marketing areas covered by various media. If your market is a 20-mile radius semi-rural area, you would not advertise property in a state-wide newspaper unless buyers normally come from outside your market area. As previously stated, except for resort and retirement communities, most real estate firms find that their buyers come from within a 20-mile radius of their offices and one-half come from even closer in. Analyzing your past buyers should reveal the market areas deserving the heaviest advertising efforts. As advertising reaches beyond this area, your coverage benefits will decrease.

Many large papers have zoned editions that allow you to zero in on your market area without having to buy coverage far beyond your market. These special area sections are primarily for display ads, as most large papers do not sectionalize their classified ads.

More than one newspaper covering your market area will produce cross-readership. Where there is both a morning and afternoon newspaper, cross-readership will be higher than if there were two morning or evening editions. Similarly, cross-readership will probably be quite high when there are two or more weekly papers covering an area. As an example, assume there are two papers in an area and each has a 100,000 circulation. With a 40,000 cross-readership, advertising in an additional paper only gives you an effective coverage of an additional 60,000. However, the cost of advertising in the second paper might be offset by its benefits. It is possible to get full advertising benefit from the second paper and avoid a big loss of cross-readership by varying ads among the papers, emphasizing different features. You can make property appeal to various groups. One reader who shows no interest in a property in one newspaper ad could be very excited about the same property advertised in another paper.

You may want to concentrate advertising dollars in a high-circulation, local paper. By focusing on a local medium, a smaller firm can appear to have a dominant presence in the local market.

In buying space in a paper or magazine, you will want to know the paid circulation. The Audit Bureau of Circulation (ABC) audits claims of publishers and publishes circulation figures.

Check your local newspapers and radio and television stations for reader or listener data. The demographic breakdown factors and numbers vary with time of day and particular programming. This material will aid you in your media selections. In selecting advertising media, don't make decisions by what your competitors use. They are more than likely acting on intutition or following the lead of someone else rather than using empirical data. Whatever medium you use, your advertising should be written for the specific medium to obtain maximum effect.

FEATURES TO ADVERTISE

In determining the emphasis of your ads, you should first analyze what type of person or family will be the likely buyer of the property and which features would appeal to that buyer. By asking the present owner which features affected his or her decision to buy and what features would most appeal to a new owner, you might get some ideas for your advertising. You want your ad to appeal to the prospective buyers.

Never write an ad on a property you have not seen. Don't take another's word. You must see the property with your own eyes to do it justice with words. Ads attracting the wrong buyers waste advertising dollars unless you are able to identify the needs of those responding and have inventory to which those buyers can be switched. Our book *Classified Secrets: Writing Real Estate Ads That Sell* (Real Estate Education Company) will help you target your ads to specific buyers.

A property could offer appeal to several types of buyers. A low-cost, two-bedroom bungalow with one bath, a single car garage and a small, fenced yard in a quiet residential neighborhood could appeal to:

• A single person
• A retired couple
• Newlyweds
• A single parent

The fenced yard could appeal to a pet owner or someone who desires to have a garden. This same home could be advertised in different ways to appeal to different buyers.

Location is often the most important feature of a home. A particularly desirable area should be in the ad heading if the location is not part of the newspaper ad category.

Any time a home has more than three bedrooms, it should be stated in the ad heading; this is a sought-after feature. Other physical features likely to attract buyers include special rooms such as dens and family rooms, the number of bedrooms, number of baths, patios, gardens, trees, size of lot and house and any special amenity a buyer might consider desirable.

For nonresidential property, lot size, zoning, structure construction and size, income, etc., would likely be of interest to a prospective buyer.

Besides physical aspects of a property, your ad can sell:

- Social approval
- Health
- Comfort
- View
- Economy
- Recreation
- Security
- Pride of ownership
- Home warranty

When a home has not sold and you feel it should have, ask your salespersons about viewer reaction. Ask what features were received positively by prospective buyers. These features will vary for different types of buyers. Features mentioned by more than one viewer should be considered for your advertising.

You might want to tell readers what is wrong with a property. Real estate is one of the few areas where a negative ad is likely to be received positively. In fact, the more you denigrate a property, the greater the appeal to fixer-upper buyers who tend to be unusual individuals. The one negative feature you should not advertise is that a *property is overpriced*. If a property is overpriced, you should not be advertising it. It is hard enough to sell competitively priced property. In fact, you are losing sight of your goals when you take an overpriced listing.

In general, you should include the price or price range in every ad. Unpriced ads get fewer responses than ads stating the price. If the price appears highly desirable, you should consider including it in the heading of your ad. Whatever price you state in your ad, the price should appear reasonable or a bargain based on your ad copy. If it doesn't, rework your copy or don't advertise the property.

Some listings sound good in print, but are difficult to sell nevertheless. An example of this would be a lot in a desirable area which is prone to flooding or has a deep ravine making construction difficult. It is unethical to take a listing you don't expect to sell in order to attract buyers for other property. You are doing a disservice to the owner, on whose behalf you are supposed to be working. It is also bad business; many buyers will not want anything to do with your firm if they feel they were tricked into contacting you.

If your firm specializes in an area or type of property, emphasize it. One firm advertises its Children's Play Center for weekend home seekers. The firm hires adults to supervise the children in a large indoor/outdoor play area with toys, video games, television (movies and cartoon tapes for children to watch), etc. They serve a hot-dog lunch for children and morning and afternoon snacks. Parents are not under pressure to get back. The firm used press releases and media ads to advertise this feature. A great many people also come to the firm because of word-of-mouth advertising. This feature differentiates the firm from its competitors and has been a very effective tool for increasing traffic.

In preparing ads, keep in mind there are no bad properties. Properties can be overpriced and mistargeted, however. Every property has had an owner in the past and will have another owner in the future. Your job is to decide who it will be and how to present the proper appeal to the likely buyer.

TESTING ADS

While we know a great deal about what makes a good ad "click" and why some ads fail, we have yet to reduce advertising to a pure science; it is still largely an art. Some of the largest advertising agencies with the best available talent will produce ads that "bomb," while advertisements written in haste sometimes prove to be phenomenally effective. Additionally, an ad can be effective in one medium and fail in another. By keeping track of calls received regarding advertisements, you can evaluate a particular ad's effectiveness and appeal. This can be enormously helpful in writing your ads.

A minor change in direct mail advertisements can change the response rate significantly. Consider test marketing different types of direct mail ads in groups of 500 to 1,000 mailings to evaluate response prior to any mass mailing. Differentiate by changing the contact names for each group in order to know which mailing brought in what percentage of response. Another response variable to be evaluated is mailing areas. Return rates differ by region.

Coupons are another excellent method of testing ad and media effectiveness. As an example, an "Open House" ad just before Christmas could include a coupon for a free toy. Different coupons in different papers will inform you of the traffic source. Another coupon variation is using them for free drawings for a major prize.

ADVERTISING AGENCIES

In planning and preparing your advertising, there are four possible courses to follow:

1. Do it yourself.
2. Hire or designate an employee to manage your advertising.
3. Employ an advertising agency.
4. Use a combination of the above.

If you are already preparing superior advertising on your own, continue to do so. Unfortunately, newspapers are full of ineffective or mediocre ads. For evaluation purposes, cut out copies of your ads and those of your competitors, eliminating firm identification, and show them to friends whose judgment you respect. If particular competitor's ads consistently rate above your firm's, you have a problem. If all rate equally, your ads are mired in mediocrity and need to be improved. You want your ads to surpass, not match, the competition's. This becomes extremely important in a slow market.

When it comes to preparing large display ads and four-color brochures, the need for professional assistance becomes apparent. You could waste thousands of dollars on mediocrity. A full-page ad in a major newspaper might cost in excess of $5,000. If the ad's effectiveness could be doubled by professional copy and artwork, failure to obtain professional assistance could prove very expensive in the long run.

You may have talent within your office for producing quality ads, but don't convert a salesperson to writing ads. You can end up losing a salesperson to gain an ad writer. It is possible to hire a freelance copywriter for one or two days a week. Paying a per diem rate on a long-term basis for your ad work will be far less costly than an hourly rate.

Most small and even medium-size brokerage firms do not place enough advertising to justify use of an advertising agency. An exception would be when the firm is handling the marketing of a large project. Firms with 100 or more salespersons should at least explore the possibility of using an ad agency; their ad volume and types of advertising could well justify it.

One simple method to locate freelance copywriters in your area is to ask advertising personnel at your local newspapers to recommend one. They will generally be cooperative, as they want your goodwill and continued advertising. You may have hired a commercial artist or photographer who has worked with copywriters in the past and can recommend someone. Copywriters will be able to recommend artists and photographers with whom they have worked well in the past. Before hiring freelance copywriters or artists, ask to see their portfolio. The best indication of what they can offer you is what they have accomplished for previous clients. Consider giving them a small job to see how well they work with you.

Some people feel that freelancers are people who really couldn't cut it with ad agencies. This is largely a misconception. Freelancers often operate independently because agencies cannot pay market value for their services. They also may have become disgruntled with many agencies' hiring and firing cycles when they gain or lose major accounts. In the Los Angeles area, many of the best and highest-paid copywriters are freelance. For important presentations, many agencies turn to freelance talent. Smaller accounts will likely obtain better quality ads from freelancers than large agencies. Large agencies tend to use less experienced staff on smaller accounts.

Even if you have your own copywriter and art director, you still have to consider media selection, ad size and timing of your advertising, etc. If these are not major problems, then in-house advertising will likely meet your needs. If they are important, consider hiring freelance professionals or an ad agency.

Some larger firms have complete in-house ad agencies. Some of these do an outstanding job. Generally these firms have hired outstanding personnel from an ad agency after reviewing what they had done for others or hired a freelancer as an employee. However, excellence is not the rule with in-house agencies; they tend to be more bridled in their advertising approaches, and mediocrity becomes the norm rather than the exception. Once a person becomes your employee, you tend to exercise greater supervision and direction over their work. When creative personnel are directed by someone who does not possess the creative talent or in-depth advertising knowledge, mediocrity results.

The one criteria you should not use in hiring a freelance worker or an ad agency is cost. Going with the low bid may turn out to be the most expensive decision of your career. Also, don't choose an agency based on friendship. If they don't meet your expectations, it is difficult to fire a friend.

Before engaging an agency, you want to find out what their other accounts are and what they have done for others. You might want to give the agency a one-time job to see how they handle it. If you have contacted several agencies, a better approach might be to have each prepare an ad or several ads for you for the same property, giving them the same parameters. Expect to pay each for their services. Some agencies will do work on speculation for larger accounts; it never hurts to ask.

In larger cities there will be a number of ad agencies that either specialize in real estate ads or have staff members with extensive real estate advertising background. Ad agencies can provide a valuable service by selecting media and arranging to buy the time or space for you. Professionals can target your ads based on buyer demographics. Agencies also understand cooperative advertising. For example, an ad for a new development could feature the name of the air-conditioning units, with their manufacturer picking up a significant portion of the ad cost.

Individuals who write their own ads tend to use the same approach after its effectiveness has worn off. Nonprofessionals are reluctant to change what was effective in the past. They blame decline in drawing power not on the ad, but on economic conditions. This is unlikely to happen with an ad agency. Creative talent is usually eager to try something new. In fact, you might find yourself having to resist change when an advertising approach is still very effective.

Ad agencies will want a written contract. The minimum period will likely be three months, although after three months, the contract will likely allow cancellation upon 30 days' notice.

Most advertising agencies receive the bulk of their compensation from media placement. For example, if an agency buys $1 million worth of TV, radio and magazine time they might receive from 10 to 16 percent commission for ad placements. However, many newspapers do not pay agency commissions. Your contract with the agency will likely provide a mark-up for noncommissioned ad placements.

Your agency contract will provide that you pay costs for out-of-agency work such as contract services. The contract might require an hourly fee in addition to or instead of a placement fee, and may require a minimum charge for smaller accounts.

Even though you use an advertising agency, you will likely have to write your classified ads in-house. Agencies will probably resist using their talent for low-dollar classified ads, because preparation costs can often exceed newspaper costs for insertion of these ads. But you don't have to start from scratch writing classified ads, see Chapter 5 for shortcuts to exceptional advertising.

If you have hired an agency, use it. Many national firms use top-notch agencies with great creative talent, yet produce mediocre advertising campaigns. We can trace this problem to clients who feel they know more about effective advertising than the professionals. People who lack background as to what makes ads effective end up overworking approval rights on advertising. A far better approach is to give the agency free rein—let them run with ad projects. If the agency fails, then reconsider your agency selection. In any event, pay your ad agency promptly. In return, you can and should expect prompt reaction to your needs.

You now know something about advertising planning and are ready to explore the media available to you. After you read Chapters 2 through 10, you will understand the media available and what each can do for you. In Chapter 11, you will put it all together in a specific advertising program.

2 The Real Estate Salesperson

The salesperson is an often overlooked but powerful advertising medium: a walking, talking and riding advertisement for himself or herself, as well as the firm. Salespeople can not only bring in business, they can increase your market presence as well. If getting the most bang for the buck is of interest to you, consider the following ideas.

NAME TAGS

A plastic, engraved name tag is an effective, low-cost advertising tool. In fact, it is so low-cost that it is all too often ignored. Your name should be in letters large enough (approximately one-half inch high) to be read at a distance of six feet. This should be followed by the firm name. If your firm name does not indicate "realty" or "real estate", you can use a large REALTOR® symbol (the block "R") if your firm is a member of the National Association of REALTORS®. The tag color should match the color scheme of your company signs. If possible, the firm's logo should be included. Name tags serve to remind all your daily contacts that you are in the real estate profession. People will ask questions about the tags, which if properly handled, could mean dollars for you. Tags act as a self-promotion, as they reinforce your name to whomever you deal with face-to-face. People will remember they talked to you by name, not "someone from your office." For just a few dollars, you can have a valuable promotional tool.

Despite their effectiveness, many salespeople resist wearing name tags. They say it makes them look unprofessional. Well, doctors at hospitals don't think it's unprofessional and neither do we. One office fines salespeople one dollar if they come into the office without their name tag. All fines collected are donated to a local charity.

UNIFORMS

Uniforms of any kind are worn for identification. You can recognize military personnel, police and waiters by the uniforms they wear. In the 1950s, Shamrock Realty had each salesperson wear a green sweater, on which was embroidered a shamrock. The firm used the shamrock motif and color on their cards, stationery and For Sale signs (figure 2.1). The vivid green sweater and shamrock motif, along with the firm's For Sale signs, gave Shamrock Realty people instant identification within their market area.

In the '60s Red Jacket Realty's salespeople wore bright red blazers. The jacket motif was also extended to the company's For Sale signs. Salespeople for a firm called McIntosh Realty wore Scottish plaid jackets.

Although some of these firms are not still in business, these ideas have continued into the '90s. Today when you see a particular mustard-colored jacket, you know immediately the wearer is from Century 21. These jackets are a walking advertisement, for which the benefits far outweigh the costs. Salespersons are even stopped in supermarkets by strangers who have real estate questions.

If you represent a one-person office and decide to wear a bright orange jacket to work every day, chances are you will quickly be classified as some kind of nut. However, if everyone in a large office wears similar distinctive attire that corresponds with the office signs and cards, you could gain a strong identification within your market area. People will quickly realize you are part of a large team. Keep in mind that in choosing a color and style you want to be distinctive, but you don't want to appear bizarre.

FIGURE 2.1 For Sale Sign Design Elements: Shamrock and Red Jacket Realty

CARDS

Business cards are a *must* in real estate sales. They are a relatively inexpensive advertising medium. As with other advertising, you must realize your competition also uses cards. An owner trying to sell a house without the aid of a broker might receive a dozen or more cards from various real estate agents. Therefore, your card can serve as your representative in a competitive situation. You want your photograph on your business cards because people can become confused as to which agent left what card. Color photos are more desirable than black and white, but any photo is better than none. Some real estate salespersons have stationery printed with their photo as well.

While cute, character drawings do not lead to ready identification and should be avoided. Also avoid the 15-year-old photograph. While great for your vanity, this won't help prospective buyers and sellers associate you with your business card.

A prospective seller or buyer with too many agents' cards can easily identify yours if the card is printed on colored card stock. Colored stock or colored ink should tie in with your office signs and stationery. Always print your firm's logo on the cards. Also include the REALTOR® block "R" if your firm is a member of the National Association of REALTORS®.

Special card stock weight and texture will also differentiate your cards from others. Some professionals prefer a very light, hard stock for their cards so they are crisp to the touch. Printing a slightly off-sized card, such as 3¾" × 1⅞", longer and slimmer than most cards, will also differentiate your card from those of other agents.

A folded business card could have the front flap cut shorter than the back. Telephone numbers can be printed on the bottom of the partially visible interior flap so they can be read without opening the card. Special effects are also possible by die-cutting the front flap of a folded business card so your photo on the interior section shows through a cut-out in the front flap of the card (figure 2.2).

FIGURE 2.2 Examples of Folded Business Cards

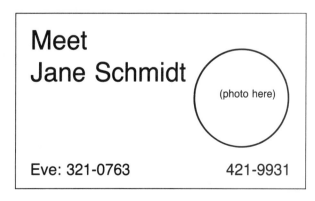

The bottom edge of the card's front flap can even be cut to resemble a city skyline, or designed to tie in with your firm's logo.

Embossed cards are expensive and, for a small firm, are probably not worth the cost. However, many large firms have huge stocks of cards printed and embossed, which makes distinctive, quality cards more affordable. (Keep in mind that after the first 1,000 cards the price should be significantly less for additional thousands). Each salesperson then uses a basic card on which to print his or her personal data and/or photograph.

Some agents have their own stationery made when their cards are printed. They simply have the card printed at the top of their stationery in the upper left-hand corner or upper center of the paper at a relatively low cost.

Some agents prefer soft plastic magnetic cards, complete with photo. The cards make great refrigerator magnets where a prospective buyer or seller can locate them—in plain sight. Agents who use magnetic cards may also use plain business cards for mass mailings, and for more casual contacts. In this way, they reserve their magnetic cards for persons contacted for listings and prospective buyers who have already been shown homes. The problem with the magnetic cards is cost, unless purchased in bulk by an entire staff.

The lower right-hand corner of your card is where people look for your office telephone number. Don't put it anyplace else. Your residence or evening telephone number should be clearly printed in the lower left-hand corner.

CAR SIGNS

Magnetic car signs are an effective and low-cost advertising tool. Car signs bring inquiries, which produce buyers and sellers from unlikely places: passersby when you park your car, neighbors when you show a property or make a listing presentation, even the employee of a local garage where you bring your car for servicing. The signs also serve to remind your own neighbors and friends that you are in the business of helping people buy and sell real estate. The most amazing inquiry we know of from a car sign was the California broker who sold a house to a highway patrol officer whom she met when he issued her a speeding ticket.

A car sign should include your office logo, if you have one, your own name, the office telephone number and your evening telephone number. At just a glance, you want the viewer to realize which office you represent. Color and design should match that of your business cards, stationery and For Sale and office signs.

As a salesperson, you want to emphasize your own name. Consider a sign such as the following:

FIGURE 2.3 Car Sign

(Logo)

Meet
Tom Brown
Clyde Realty
476-8200
Eve: 476-9210

The sign emphasizes the name of the salesperson, shows the firm name and logo design, and includes the REALTOR® block "R" and office and home numbers. Cost can be low if you order multiple sets, as most of the expense in these plastic signs is associated with set-up costs. If you want to realize savings, negotiate directly with a firm that has its own vacuum press or silkscreen operation, and not the agent or dealer who orders the signs for you. Part of your order may include a third rear sign if you own a station wagon, van or square-trunk vehicle for additional effective advertising in city traffic. For those vehicles not suited for a rear sign, a converted bicycle rack will serve to hold the third sign on the trunk. Several commercial signs like this are already available on the market.

Personalized license plates are just another sign (figure 2.4). They are small, but every little bit helps.

FIGURE 2.4 Personalized License Plates

| ABC RLTY | RE SALE | SIMON RE | SELL RE |

CAR COLORS

When you see a pink Cadillac, you instantly know that the car's owner sells Mary Kay Cosmetics. This same identification is possible with real estate firms. A fleet of automobiles painted the same unusual color would provide instant identification within your community. For instance, ten purple Mercedes-

Benzes in a community of 20,000 people would soon make many associate those cars with your firm. Of course, each car should display matching magnetic signs, and your chosen color should tie in with your signs and calling cards. There's only one problem; if you suggest that your salespeople have their Mercedes-Benzes repainted some bold color, you're liable to be a candidate for stoning or an otherwise early demise. To achieve color identification of your cars, you must either supply the cars or talk your salespeople into wanting purple automobiles.

Some property management firms supply salaried managers with specially painted vehicles rather than reimburse them for their mileage. Land companies have made rental payments on autos when their salespeople reached certain quotas. Supplying cars would be out of the question for most real estate firms because of cost.

You could offer an incentive to get salespersons to repaint their cars. As an example, an office could offer a higher commission schedule for salespeople who paint their automobiles, plus pay to paint and repaint when a vehicle is ready for a trade-in.

PUBLIC SPEAKING

Public speaking is verbal advertising. It offers you the opportunity to promote yourself as an expert.

Service organizations such as Rotary, Soroptimist, Kiwanis, etc., are always looking for speakers. Once you speak at one group, you can expect to receive invitations from other groups.

Some topics of interest to your listeners for public presentations, could be:

- My crystal ball—The real estate market in Westhaven for the coming 12 months
- Real estate—The last tax shelter
- Real estate investment opportunities in a down market
- Beware the charlatans (Buyers using colored stones, uncut diamonds, worthless paper, subordination clauses, etc.)
- The economic effect on the community of (a particular new development)

By offering to provide your listeners with additional material, you can easily obtain their business cards or names and addresses, which are excellent for future contacts. Remember, you have sold yourself as an expert already, so these contacts can be extremely valuable.

Similar talks can be given as seminars at local community colleges. Also, consider teaching a real estate class at your local community college. Teaching can go a long way toward establishing your reputation as an expert.

NEWSPAPER COLUMNS

Writing a weekly column for a local newspaper can help you develop a reputation as a real estate expert within your community. After seeing your photograph in the column week after week, potential clients will recognize you as an "authority," not just another real estate salesperson.

If you are interested in writing a column, prepare several samples to present to the newspaper. They should be written on subjects of interest to the average reader. You should agree to supply the column in a timely fashion at no cost to the paper.

To present professional material, some column writers hire a local public relations firm or freelance writer to put their thoughts in a presentable order.

Subject matter for your column could be economic trends, advantages of refinancing, changes in tax laws, the tax effect of a sale, the likely effect of a new development, explanation of required seller disclosures, etc.

3 Your Office Presence

Your office signs, decor, equipment and policies can be effective in promoting new business and in encouraging visitors to deal with your firm.

LOGOS

The larger the marketplace, the more important it is to establish your firm's identity.

A logo is a unique design, symbol or signature used as your firm's identifying mark. A good logo would be distinctively designed so it brings business to you, not to your competitor. A logo similar to your competitor's could also subject you to a costly lawsuit and possible damages. While it should be memorable and easily identifiable at a glance, your firm's logo should also be relatively clear and simple so it can be used on your signs, stationery and business cards. Always spell out your name and the name of your firm with every identification. Some logos are simply firm names stylized or included within the design. If a logo is too cluttered, it cannot be identified at a distance. Distance identification is particularly important when using a logo on your For Sale signs.

Your talent is in real estate; a logo designer's talent is in logos. Why waste your time doing what someone else is trained to do? Have your logo prepared by a professional after you have made a selection from reviewing two or three designers' sample illustrations.

If your firm uses a coined name (formed from acronyms or other unusual word combinations), be careful it doesn't mean something unpleasant in another language. One real estate firm located in a heavily Hispanic community opened its offices with a manufactured logo taken from the names of two principals. Unfortunately, the name had a particularly vulgar meaning in Spanish. Changing the name of the firm necessitated changing signs and stationery. It proved to be a costly mistake.

FIGURE 3.1   Examples of Distinctive Real Estate Firm Logos

Sources: Landmark Real Estate, Maryellen Hill & Associates, Rothermund Rudman Incorporated, REALTORS®, Wall Street West Real Estate. Reprinted with permission.

OFFICE SIGNS AND DISPLAYS

Unless the style and color of your office sign is controlled by your lessor or by local sign ordinances, it should match the logo, color and style of your office For Sale signs, stationery and calling cards. You want people to recognize at a glance that the office belongs to your firm.

Many offices use marquees or the common yellow electric billboard type signs with movable black plastic letters. These signs can be used to promote particular properties. Choose properties that appear to be desirable in price, but remember to change these signs weekly, as they are effective advertising and will bring in walk-ins. Around $500 for a yellow lighted billboard will earn back your investment many times in buyers you wouldn't otherwise have met.

If your community has a strict sign control ordinance, you might consider hanging large American and state flags outside your office or above the building. Cities hesitate applying sign ordinances to flags—and flags do draw attention. Flag flying can also include foreign ones. Some offices in the Southwest fly both the American and Canadian flags due to the great influx of north-of-the-border visitors.

When a firm's name is on a building, it does not necessarily mean that firm is the owner of the building. The firm more likely used its economic clout to place the name on the building. Naming a building can be a negotiable issue when contracting for a significant portion of office space on a long-term lease. If you are a major tenant in a building with no name or if the building is named after the owner, who does not have a business on the premises, you should consider negotiating with the management company to name the building after your firm. Having the name gives you an opportunity for further visual recognition as to your location with an additional sign, often a large one, and it also provides your firm with a public image of strength and permanence.

In negotiating a lease, consider including a provision giving your office an exclusive right to sell the property for a stated period of time if it is placed on the market. It certainly won't help your firm's public image if a competitor's For Sale sign adorns your office building, not to mention how devastating this could be to your self-esteem.

Heavy foot traffic in front of an office display window demands a display of color photos with brief details and prices of properties offered. You may be able to use property briefs (See Chapter 9) for the window displays by pasting color photos over the drawings. Details should be written similarly to a classified ad with ample descriptive adjectives. You want enough information to get the reader's attention, interest and desire to make him or her run, not walk, across your threshold.

Updating window photo displays is important. Faded, discolored and dusty displays show they have been in the window a long time—this is worse than no display at all. You want the window display to carry the image of success, not failure.

If you are a salesperson, offer to take responsibility for the window displays if they are in poor shape. Of course, the displays would then feature your own listings. Window positions should be changed on property displays held over from month to month. Several commercial window display racks are available without resorting to wires, paper clips and tape. These displays should be no higher than about 50 inches from the floor so passersby can see into your office.

Another source of sign displays are vacant storefronts. Ask your landlord if you can use vacant units for displays. Chances are you can obtain valuable free display space. You don't always have to pay for what you get!

Many years ago, a Madison, Wisconsin, broker placed a fish tank in his office display window with lights, filters, weeds and snails but not one fish! He posted a sign, *Piscus Afric non vid (African Invisible Fish)—Very Rare.* Passersby stared at the tank looking for fish, but the tank did not contribute to listings or sales. A far better approach would have been to use an electronic, moving message sign giving details of a number of properties. Electronic signs are particularly valuable when an office is located on a corner near a bus stop or traffic light. Easy to program, the signs vary in time limits as to "Times Square" types of messages. Some message sequences go on for more than ten minutes. The signs are approximately nine inches high and four feet to six feet in length. A local sign company can order one for you.

Your office waiting room should be stocked with office listings, listing briefs, a listing presentation book, and real estate journals and brochures—not general magazines. When preferred reading material is not handy, people will read what is available.

OFFICE DECOR

Your business days don't have to end after dark during winter months; however, your drop-in business will evaporate after dark if your office and parking area are not well-lit. Passersby should be able to clearly see people inside your office, and the parking area should be brightly lighted so people don't consider it a hazard.

The office exterior is an advertisement for what is inside and should appear as inviting as possible. Where applicable, flowers and plantings confer a friendly appearance. This can extend to your office decor, which is your interior advertising. Office decor can convey a positive or negative image. Poorly lighted areas, dirty walls and floors and mismatched furniture work to give the impression of an unsuccessful office and a second-rate staff. On the other hand, computers visible on entry help set an up-to-date image.

The generous use of wood paneling in closing rooms and private offices carries a strong image of reliability. Solid wood paneling or wainscoting provides an image of strength. Wooden bookcases with glass doors are also a valuable image asset. Large antique desks sell at a premium and, although expensive, are worth the image they convey. Older quality wooden furniture and well-worn leather chairs convey *strength*, and can often be purchased for less money than the lowest priced new steel and plastic furnishings.

Plaques and suitably framed awards, diplomas and professional designations should be in full view. If you treat your achievements as being valuable, others will as well. Old English prints could be also considered for wall decor; they carry a dignified, professional image. Cheap accessories convey the image you won't be in business very long.

Just as office decor helps to sell your office and you as a professional, your attire is a personal advertisement. Don't try to be a trend-setter. Your overall appearance should be consistent with other business professionals in your area (i.e., the clients you wish to attract).

"800" NUMBERS

Brokers selling retirement, vacation and investment properties frequently spend a significant portion of the advertising budget outside their local marketing area. Some advertisements indicate the reader can call collect. However, people hesitate to make such calls, as they feel an obligation, or sense they are being unfair in saddling someone with a telephone charge. These ads result in few calls. Many callers will actually pay their own long distance charges despite the invitation to call collect.

The effectiveness of advertising outside your local area can be multiplied by simply including an "800" number. Most people realize an "800" number does not cost the caller and they don't hesitate to use it; they don't have to go through operators to let them know the person they are calling should pay for their call. Although use of "800" numbers is not free, their effectiveness has been proven by the fact that we know of relatively few brokers who have canceled the use of such service.

There are *interstate* and *intrastate* "800" numbering systems. A basic installation fee for either could cost around $350. There is also a monthly fee from approximately $25 to $70, and also per-hour charges. Per-hour charges vary by time of day as well as type of service, and can cost from approximately $9 to $20 per hour. For information on specific costs call your long-distance telephone company's customer service department.

If your competitors use "800" numbers and you're not, they have a competitive edge. While the cost of an "800" number might seem high, consider the costs of other advertising media. You will quickly realize that, even if they can increase the effectiveness of your advertising just 25 percent, "800" numbers will be a bargain. Your "800" number should be displayed in large print in your advertising, mailings and business card. Don't hide this competitive advantage; flaunt it.

TELEPHONE ANSWERING MACHINES

You will get office calls before and after normal hours. Often, these calls will be from persons calling on advertisements; if they fail to make contact with you they will call a competitor about another ad. You don't want to risk losing these callers. Mechanical sounding messages turn many people off. Some won't even leave a message. Yet the right message can increase the likelihood of a response and serve to create a positive image for you and your firm.

For a possible office answering machine message, consider the following:

This is Clyde Realty at Sixth and Main. While our office is closed now, please don't hang up. If you would like to talk right now to a representive from Clyde Realty, call either 555-9840 or 555-7681, that's 555-9840 or 555-7681, or leave a message after the tone and a Clyde Realty salesperson will get back to you.

While the message is long, it repeats two of the salesperson's home numbers. (These can be rotated.) Clyde Realty is mentioned three times and we have given the location of the office.

Remember the old radio program of the '40s, "Blondie"? It began with, "Ah! Ah! Ah! Ah! Don't touch that dial!" This was an effective approach in keeping listeners interested, and you can do the same on your answering machine:

Ah! Ah! Ah! Ah! Don't hang up! Sure I'm a machine but I work for real people at Clyde Realty, and you can be talking with one of Clyde Realty's salespeople in less than one minute. Call 555-8379 or 555-9376, that's 555-8379 or 555-9376. Or, if you want to leave a message after the tone, a Clyde Realty salesperson will get back to you soon.

Again, the above message mentions Clyde Realty three times.

In recording your message, use a natural, happy tone of voice and speak slowly. Message emphasis should be on your firm name and any telephone numbers to call. Always repeat the numbers slowly.

Your salespeople will each need a telephone answering machine at home. While they receive responses from the office messages, cards, ads and sign strips, salespeople won't always be at home to field calls.

Consider the following message for home use:

Hi! I'm the answering machine of Judy Jones. Don't hang up because I'm the friendliest answering machine you will ever talk to. Judy Jones is the nicest salesperson at Clyde Realty, and I know Judy can meet your real estate needs, but you must leave a message for her to help you. So, I will make a beep and then you get to talk, and Judy will get back to you. Now, Judy, she's a real person!

While the message is on the cute side, it will be remembered. Also, it's the kind of message that invites a reply. It gives strong name identification as "Judy Jones" is repeated twice, and "Judy" three times. A caller would have difficulty not replying to this message.

Most new answering machines will indicate how many calls were received—you will know your success rate from the number of responses. Your success rate would be the percentage of callers leaving messages. This gives you the opportunity to test your message and modify it to give you improved results in terms of names and numbers given.

SALES CONTESTS

Sales contests are really promotions directed toward your own staff for the purpose of motivating them to reach higher goals. Prospective buyers and sellers are not the only parties to be reached through advertising.

An effective sales promotion must dangle a carrot that your salespeople desire—something they really want, but wouldn't buy for themselves because other obligations take priority. A very prestigious watch, set of Ping golf clubs, a short vacation at a luxury location, or even a one-year lease on a luxury automobile make good sales incentives.

It is not enough to simply offer a desirable prize. The prize must be awarded for reaching a possible goal. Never put your salespeople in competition with one another; they should be in competition with themselves. As an example, if you offered a single prize for the largest number of escrows closed, on largest dollar volume of sales, etc., there could be only one winner. Salespeople would not be motivated by the successes of fellow salespeople, they would instead resent the success. A single prize is an invitation for lousy office moral and a feeling of "me" rather than the team feeling of "us."

Salespeople must be constantly reminded of the prize. Office posters should feature Hawaii if the prize is a week in Hawaii. Enlarged color pictures of prizes are effective, but not as much as having the prize displayed in the office. One office displayed a mannequin wearing a mink jacket. Salespeople could feel the jacket as they walked by, and employees wives actually came to the office to try it on. This October-to-January sales promotional period resulted in three of ten salespersons reaching the goal and each earning a mink jacket. The office had exceptional sales during what was normally the worst quarter of the year. Even those who did not earn a jacket were winners. If a fur jacket is not desirable in your area, a few minutes' reflection should give you a winner, perhaps a cruise.

If the contest prize is a vacation, schedule the trip (never more than one week) during a slow time of the year of your business. You don't want to send a salesperson away during a period of great activity. This defeats the purpose of the contest—to increase sales.

One recreational land sales office offered a one-year lease on a Range Rover as a promotion prize in meeting a sales goal. The Range Rover was parked in a prime space at the office surrounded by velvet rope. This desirable gift became a power presentation in full view daily for all the salespeople.

Effective sales promotion should consider spousal support. A spouse who wants a prize can be a great motivator by encouraging rather than discouraging extra working hours. To get the message across, a good time to announce sales contests is at office social functions when spouses are present. One large office sends its salespeople special delivery letters announcing sales incentive programs. The spouse will want to know what the letter is about, so the excitement about the program builds from their interest.

When a particular sale is important to a firm, such as a builder's home where the sale means more listings, an office can encourage a special sales effort by offering cash (spiff), or preferably merchandise. During a seller's market, when just about anything is saleable, salespeople can be encouraged with an incentive for obtaining listings in desirable areas within 110 percent of the appraised value.

A side benefit of sales promotions with significant prizes is higher moral and a reduced rate of turnover in successful salespeople. Competitors offering higher commission rates will have greater difficulty in stealing away your salespeople. As for your staff, internal sales promotions serve to help salespeople achieve their personal best.

SALESPERSON RECRUITMENT ADS

One of the best recruitment advertising techniques is simple word-of-mouth advertising. You should explain to salespeople your reasons for increasing the staff and enlist their help in recruitment. Every real estate salesperson knows salespeople in other firms, often socially as well as through business dealings. They also know which salespeople are not happy with particular brokers. A side benefit of hiring through referrals is that the salesperson who brings in the new salesperson will feel a duty to be the new salesperson's mentor until he or she becomes familiar with the office and its policies.

One broker, who regularly uses her own staff to recruit new salespeople, gives a very nice gift and thank-you note to the salesperson whose recruit just closed his or her first sale.

Many firms try to obtain salespeople by offering a higher commission rate than is generally offered in the area. We believe this approach is unwise. This type of salesperson will likely be marginal in sales and will be the first to leave should someone else offer more. A far better approach is to offer a professional office with broker and salesperson success.

Salesperson recruitment ads can be placed in any media, although most people looking for positions check the local newspapers classified ads. You can also prepare fliers for distribution at personnel offices advertising positions available to new retirees as well as those terminated due to business conditions.

Many firms advertise an open house where they speak about the firm, licensing requirements, training programs and details of the job. It is very effective to have several fairly recently licensed employees talk about their experiences and answer questions.

For examples of salesperson recruitment mailers and fliers, see figure 3.2.

Some effective classified recruitment ads are shown in figure 3.3. A secondary benefit to these ads is that the ads present a very professional view of your firm. The first ad is aimed at readers who are not currently licensed real estate agents, as well as new licensees. The last two ads are for a successful sales agent, not a new licensee. These ads give very little information; their purpose is simply to have an opportunity to meet a salesperson interested in making a change.

For additional recruitment ads, see the "Charity Ads and Sponsorship" section in Chapter 8.

FOR SALE SIGNS

For Sale signs or lawn signs are by far your most cost-effective advertisement. In many cases, your sign on a property will bring in more and better buyer contacts than will costly newspaper ads.

FIGURE 3.2 Salesperson Recruitment Mailers and Fliers

> **Join Us for Real Estate Career Night**
>
> • Learn how many people have found new direction in their lives through real estate.
>
> • Learn the benefits that a professional career in real estate offers:
>
>   • The joy of helping others
>
>   • The independence of planning your own work
>
>   • Financial rewards directly related to your success in helping meet housing needs
>
>   • Constant mental stimulation
>
> If you are a retiree, a homemaker reentering the work force, a recent graduate or simply interested in a career change, this is your opportunity to learn how a real estate career meets your needs, and to ask any questions you might have.
>
> *[Thursday, April 8th]*
> *[7:00 P.M.]*
> *[Clyde Realty]*
> *[473 N. Main]*
>
> *[R.S.V.P]* *[555-8200]*

Your For Sale signs should include your firm name, logo and telephone number. The words *for sale* or *offered by* are not really needed, but are included by most firms. The lettering should be legible from a distance of at least 100 feet. If they are not, the size or style of lettering, or the size of your sign or colors, or both, need to be changed.

The ten most legible sign color combinations in order of preference, are:

1. Black letters, yellow background
2. Black letters, white background
3. Yellow letters, black background
4. White letters, black background
5. Blue letters, white background
6. White letters, blue background

FIGURE 3.2 Salesperson Recruitment Mailers and Fliers (continued)

[Date]

_____
_____
_____

Dear _____ :

I understand you [are currently enrolled in a real estate license preparatory course] [have applied to take your real estate salesperson's examination]. I wish you success and I hope you find real estate as personally rewarding a career as many of us have.

[Clyde Realty] is looking for people who are sincerely seeking a career and not just a job. People who want professional growth so they can meet the needs of others; people with integrity and desire.

If you feel your goals are compatible with ours, I would like to meet with you to discuss various career options, and to let you learn about us as we learn about you.

Please call me for a personal appointment.

Sincerely,

_____

Source: *Power Real Estate Letters.* Copyright 1990, Dearborn Financial Publishing, Inc., Chicago.

7. Blue letters, yellow background
8. Yellow letters, blue background
9. Green letters, white background
10. White letters, green background

If the color of your signs blends in with the background (house or landscaping), you should use an additional color for a one-inch contrasting color border around the sign.

The colors and design of your signs should match those of your office signs, cards and stationery. You want a single glance to tell the drive-by prospect your office is representing the seller.

Desirable, special features can be advertised on your sign with an added rider strip at the top of the sign. These features can include a pool, number of bedrooms, air-conditioning, a price reduction, an assumable loan, low down-payment, owner financing available, or a recently remodeled property. An

FIGURE 3.2   Salesperson Recruitment Mailers and Fliers (continued)

Tired of Retired?

If you like people, are of good moral character and are not afraid to start a new career, I would like to hear from you.

I can offer you the personal satisfaction of helping others, a feeling of self-worth working in an independent environment, mental stimulation and financial rewards earned by your success. After a short license training program, we will work with you and guide you on your career.

Interested? Then call me today so we can meet and discuss your career in real estate.

[*Tom Flynn*]
[*General Manager*]
[*555-8200*]   [*Clyde Realty*]

NOTE: *This flier can be posted at retirement communities and senior centers as well as used as a mailing piece.*

Source: *Power Real Estate Letters.* Copyright 1990, Dearborn Financial Publishing, Inc., Chicago.

assortment of rider strips are available through real estate supply stores.

A lower strip on your signs should list an evening telephone number, generally the home number of the listing agent such as seen in figure 3.4.

When a property is sold, you want a Sold rider on the sign. This rider is an advertisement of your success and is valuable in obtaining additional listings. To get maximum benefit of the Sold rider, leave the sign up until the new owner takes possession.

Your For Sale signs should be distinctive from the signs of other firms. You don't want someone calling your competitors for information on one of your listings because your firm's signs resemble their signs.

Doug Malouf, one of Australia's most successful brokers, obtained maximum impact from his signs by following Earl Nightingale's advice, "Find out what everyone else is doing and do something totally different." While discreet 18″ × 24″ signs

FIGURE 3.3 Salesperson Recruitment Classified Advertisements

Real Estate
A Profession—Not a Job

We are looking for a person who sincerely wants to help people. Someone who believes in the importance of personal integrity. What we have to offer is an opportunity to work with others sharing similar values, and to achieve your personal goals. Want to know more? Call Tom Hendricks at:

Clyde Realty   **555-8200**

Real Estate Sales
and We Mean Sales

Our promotional program has resulted in more activity than our present staff can handle. If you are a professional with a proven record, you could be the person we are looking for. Call me today if professionalism and success are important to you.

Tom Higgins

Clyde Realty   **555-8200**

Real Estate Salespersons

Are you a dedicated professional? Do you want a career rather than a job? We are a professional office where the success of our sales-people comes second only to the needs of our clients. If you want a long-term relationship you can be proud of in a positive and support-ive environment, we would like to meet with you to discuss your future. Please call John Morris at:

Clyde Realty   **555-8200**

---

were pretty much a standard size in For Sale signs in his area, Doug went with a giant 36″ × 48″ sign that he set vertically rather than horizontally. One glance at his signs tells the viewer it is a Dougmal Real Estate listing.

Several U.S. firms have now gone to oversize signs with

FIGURE 3.4   For Sale Sign with Rider Strip

huge, wooden beam holders that take a two-man crew to erect (figure 3.5). Such signs and posts are impressive and especially so when the firm is dominant in their market. A problem with these large signs is that they often take several days to erect. This can be solved by using a standard metal stake sign in the interim. The advantage of the metal stake signs is they are easy to set and remove. Also, the sign can be affixed to the stake quickly and securely with nuts and bolts.

Some exclusive residential communities limit sign size, colors and even print styles. By only allowing a small neutral colored sign without logo or special riders, you lose the ability to distinguish your firm from others with your signage. Most areas of the country have few if any limitations on For Sale signs, which allows you to distinguish your firm by your signs' design.

As you can see from figure 3.6, a rectangular design is not a requirement. Special signs can be cut from one-half inch exterior or marine plywood, and any good silk-screen shop can paint them for you. The signs should be finished with a good, clear coat of sealer for protection from the weather.

FIGURE 3.5   Sign on Hinged Post

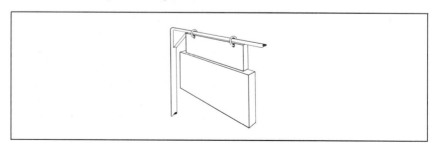

FIGURE 3.6 Unique Sign Designs

When you have a commercial lot or any unusually large lot or one that has desirable zoning, a special sign should be made for the lot. While billboard size would be great for your firm's image it would be costly and likely lead to problems because of local sign ordinances. You may be permitted to put up a 4′ by 8′ sign made of a standard sheet of five-eighths inch exterior plywood. It should be bolted to 6″ × 6″ treated wood posts (in a good wind, a 4″ × 4″ post could give way). Even with 6″ × 6″ supports, a rear brace is advisable for signs posted in an open area (figure 3.7). Depending upon the area, chances are you can get such a sign painted and erected for about $200.

When a property is sold, put a Sold banner across your large sign and leave it there. The sign might stay for years advertising your success.

A great many sign attachments are available to hold fliers describing the property or brochures that include information on other properties. To be effective, these holders must clearly indicate they contain information on the property. Most real estate supply stores carry an assortment of brochure or flier holders that attach to For Sale signs.

FIGURE 3.7   Sign with Rear Support Brace

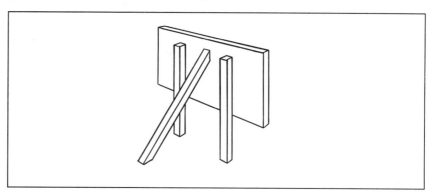

"TALKING" SIGNS

"Talking" house signs are gaining popularity. Equipped with low-powered radio transmitters, they tell the listener about the house. The message is like a printed ad in that it includes the descriptive adjectives to make the listener want to see the interior of the home. The rider strip on the For Sale sign identifies the house as a "talking house" and directs the listener to a specific radio station (e.g., 680AM).

The message is usually one or two minutes long, and plays on a continous-loop audiocasette.

The radio transmitters come in FM or AM models. FM models have a range of 75 to 200 feet and the AM models range from 100 to 250 feet. The AM transmitters are generally preferred because of greater range. Prices vary from about $150 to $800, but the price per listing is really quite low, because the machines last for years. The quality of the machine is not necessarily related to the price. Some machines use separate tape players and transmitters, while others are integrated, which seems to make the most sense. Installation is simple: you just plug it in, set the frequency and hit the *on* button. Some machines come with alternative battery packs, which is a desirable feature. You want to set a frequency that is a dead spot on your local radio band. Homeowners won't even realize their home is advertising itself 24 hours a day, as the machine makes no noise.

You might consider using a local radio personality with a distinctive voice for your message. You should take the same time in composing your message as you would in writing an ad. You must keep in mind that your message isn't to sell, only to paint a word picture that will encourage action, which will hopefully be a call for an appointment.

The following is an example of such a message:

This 3-bedroom, 2½-bath Mediterranean-style residence was designed by Hubert Klingman and built by Corwin Builders. The home features a bright, open floor plan and is decorated in the neutral earth tones of the Southwest. You will love the rich Berber carpeting and fine imported tile. The sumptuous master suite features walk-in his-and-hers closets and a Grecian tile bath with Jacuzzi. The greenhouse window in the breakfast room looks out over the patio and sparkling pool with its own hot spa that's perfect for relaxing evenings at home. Priced at under $200,000, this exceptional value warrants your immediate attention.

Don't tell listeners the home has a two-car garage; they know this. Give the price if it is competitive.

When you get a call on a talking house sign, the caller will be half-sold already. They like the house from the outside, they like the area and are interested in the features mentioned. They have really sold themselves with your nonthreatening message.

An advantage of having talking signs before your competition has them is that it gives your office listing clout. Owners are impressed with the talking sign idea. It also can get your firm favorable publicity with a press release in your local papers.

4

Classified and Display Advertising

The largest part of the advertising budget for over 90 percent of real estate firms is spent on classified and display advertising in newspapers and magazines. The greater portion of this amount, for most general brokerage firms, is spent on advertising in the classified columns. Display ads are, however, the preferred type of advertising for new developments. Broker advertising is concentrated in classified and display ads simply because they are effective.

THE CLASSIFIED READER

Generally, the purpose of classified ads is to interest potential buyers in particular properties. Classified ads also work to promote your company. When certain styles or logos are repeatedly printed it indicates that your firm has a significant presence in the marketplace. The institutional affect allows your ads to play a role in obtaining listings and producing contacts for you regarding other real estate needs. Classified ads differ from other media in that the reader actually seeks out ads, hoping a property will meet his or her needs.

House-hunters read classified ads. In a 1989 study, the Newspaper Advertising Bureau found that 83 percent of recent homebuyers had read the classified section in their search for a new residence. Of these, four out of five read the Sunday editions of classified ads and one-half checked daily classified sections. Ten percent of homebuyers indicated their house hunting concentrated around classified ads, and seven out of ten buyers made calls or visited an open house after reading the classifieds. The remaining house-hunters used another single means or a combination of means in locating homes. Nine of ten buyers occasionally checked classified ads after having made a purchase. Homeowners who live in a home ten years or less tend to read classified ads more frequently than those who remain in their residence for a longer period. Nonbuyers regularly check the classifieds, and often relate ad information to others who are in the market for homes.

Newspaper Advertising Bureau suggests abbreviations, technical terms and acronyms be avoided when writing ads, since it confuses readers. The bureau stated that areas of white space (slugs) are not used often enough in classified advertising. Slugs increase readability by making ads stand out on the printed page. According to the bureau, 9 percent of classified ad readers dismiss ads that do not look good or are difficult to read.

Area and price should be included in advertisements. Some 22 percent of readers dismiss ads when the area is not given or they do not consider the area desirable. Of ad readers, 36 percent will not inquire about a home if the price is either not stated in the ad or is considered too high. People will not respond to ads that exclude price or price range because they do not want to be embarrassed by calling on property priced beyond their means. This applies to luxury homes as well as more modest housing. Eliminating price information simply reduces the effectiveness of your ads. If you are ashamed to state a high price, you shouldn't be advertising the property. Instead, return the listing to the owner or get it more competitively priced. Also, never state "asking" or "submit all offers" in your ads. Readers will get the message the asking price is too high.

The Newspaper Advertising Bureau survey indicated that men are more interested in financial matters (price and terms), while women showed greater interest in location and special features. Of readers surveyed, 13 percent indicated they do not inquire on ads that are not specific enough. The study revealed homebuyers feel ads should include the following:

- Features of the home and community
- Financing
- Number of bedrooms and baths
- Price
- Some ideas as to location
- Anything else of special interest

We can understand from this data why bare-bones ads fail to elicit any significant response. A feature worth mentioning in an ad should be spelled out clearly with adjectives to present a positive mental picture of that feature. Inane descriptions such as "cute as a bug's ear" should be avoided. Keep in mind that in writing ads you are selling far more than a structure with a piece of ground; you're selling security, love and a future life.

In placing a classified ad, ask yourself, "under what newspaper category would a likely buyer look?" For instance, if a two-acre property were zoned for horses, this could likely be a feature attractive to many buyers. A "horse property" category would be the proper placement for this type of ad. However, the same property could be advertised under "acreage" (if say, the house were old and likely to be demolished). "Livable" and "usable as a residence or guest house" could be a positive advertised feature under the same "acreage" heading. The property may also fit "homes with acreage" and suburban categories of the newspaper. Similarly, a motel might be advertised under "business opportunities" or "investment property." Consider where most similar properties are advertised when making your decision to place an ad.

CLASSIFIED STYLES

Classified ads come in one color—black. Most newspapers will allow you to use special signature cuts or logos. Some will not allow reverse cuts (white on black) because the excessive use of ink creates a messy newspaper, but most papers will allow reverse logos with some size limitations.

Some newspapers have special border cuts available to make your ads stand out from others. Newspaper stock cuts are available ranging from the American flag to cartoon-like drawings for use in advertisements.

Only a limited choice of type styles is available for classified ads. Many papers allow one type style in several sizes. While serif type styles are generally regarded as more readable, there seems to be a trend away from using them. Serif faces are the one with little "tails" under each letter used in most news sections and books. Whatever type face you use, avoid capitalizing the entire ad body because it makes the ad more difficult to read. A better approach would be to use large, upper and lower case letters with only the first letter of each word capitalized in the ad heading and only the first word of each sentence capitalized in the body of the ad.

You want your firm's ads to stand out. You can accomplish this with borders, logos or special cuts, and a better use of headings and white space to grab the attention of readers. White space is very important in papers restricting use of special cuts and type styles that would otherwise give your ads distinction. White space is also valuable where more than one property is advertised in the same ad. Don't run the ad copy of the different properties together. Slugs will attract the reader's attention to the fact you are advertising a group of properties.

Classified ads from an Australian firm (designed by Gordon Wearing-Smith from Ampersand Advertising and Marketing

FIGURE 4.1 Distinctive Classified Ads

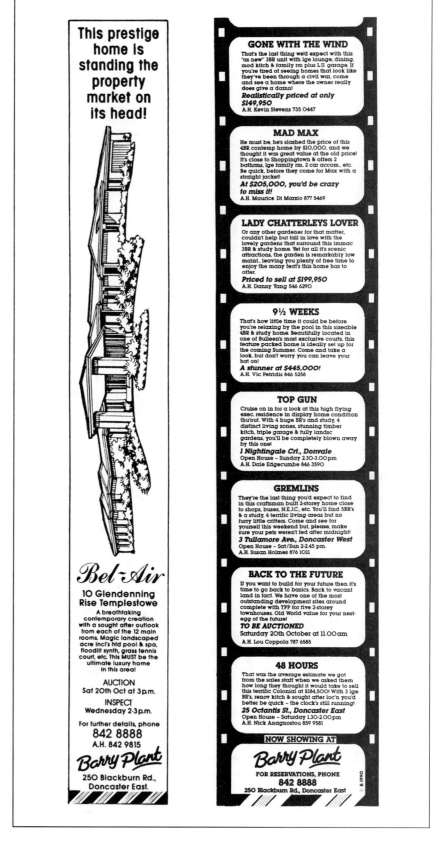

Source: Ampersand Advertising and Marketing, Kallista, Australia. Reprinted with permission.

FIGURE 4.2 Sample Line Drawing for Ad

in Kallista, Australia) are featured in figure 4.1). The ads are excellent examples of how to make your classifieds stand out. Such an approach is possible in newspapers that allow special cuts in advertisements.

A line drawing of the advertised home really makes it a display ad within the classified columns. Figure 4.2 shows how an effective line drawing need not take a great deal of space. Small line drawings such as this can be effectively used in large block classified ads as well as single-column ads.

Many brokers block all classified ads together in one large ad. They can be one-fourth, one-half or even full-page ads, which are very impressive in showing that a firm has many listings. This type of ad layout serves as a strong tool to obtain listings. However, if such an ad is not placed under the proper category for all the homes listed, interested buyers might miss some properties.

Using a computer to set up your ad copy allows you to easily duplicate the column size of your local newspaper. To do this, set your margins to include the same number of letters (including spaces) as a column line in the classified. This valuable tool will not only help you in figuring the ad cost in advance but also will help you to eliminate "widows" (a last line of copy made up of a single word or part of a word). Solutions to a widow are shortening or better yet, adding descriptive wording or features to strengthen the ad.

Avoid most abbreviations; they confuse the reader. Abbreviated words lack impact in your ads. However, abbreviations such as "BR" for bedroom and numerals rather than words assist in readability and save space.

In a seller's market, you will get an excellent response even to mediocre ads. Many brokers think they write excellent ads because of positive responses when in fact, even the poorest ads will bring calls. Better ads bring greater response and more qualified buyers. The need for quality ads becomes critical during a buyer's market because you are competing with many sellers for a much more limited pool of buyers.

ATTENTION-GRABBING HEADS

Ads must be read to have any effect; to accomplish this, we use headings. Quality headings either state a feature of a property or grab the attention of readers, practically forcing them to read the ad. Feature headings are more desirable when that feature is a prime consideration by ad hunters. A desirable location is very often the most important feature of an ad. If the newspaper uses the desirable location in the ad category heading, it would be redundant to repeat the location in the ad. If a desirable area or development is not spelled out in the newspaper category heading, then the location should be predominantly displayed in the ad, preferably in the ad heading.

The ads in figure 4.3 use features to grab the reader's attention.

Curiosity is a strong motivator in human behavior. An unexpected ad heading can act as a magnet to draw the reader's attention to the ad body. We can use the very human trait of curiosity to our advantage. The ads in figure 4.4 were designed to catch the reader's eye and intrigue him or her to find out what the ad is all about.

YOUR READER'S NEEDS

Successful advertising responds to the needs and desires that motivate people. You must capture the reader's imagination so that he or she will be intrigued enough to make that call.

Nostalgia

Nostalgia of a real or imaginary past can be a very effective advertising tool. Reviving stored memories in a positive frame can have a tremendous effect on the reader's perception of the property. The ads in figure 4.5 utilize nostalgia to motivate the reader:

FIGURE 4.3 Feature-Oriented Classified Ads

Dutch Colonial— 5BR

Since the children left to find themselves, the owners have been rattling around in this Westhaven home that is way too large for their needs. They are even having trouble finding each other, as there are 11 rooms. Incidentally, the price works out to only $12,000 per room.

Clyde Realty   **476-8200**

This ad forces the reader to compute the total price.

Beverly Hills Address

and a 3BR, 2-bath American Colonial with family room and double garage are available but

Without the Price

That's right. The most impressive address imaginable at only $395,000.

Clyde Realty   **476-8200**

This ad sells the home's address, not the home itself. You can also use the name of a prestigious street or subdivision.

24 Units—Westwood

These are well-maintained 2BR units that have no rent control. There is a tenant waiting list, and this property will show a positive cash flow after a 25 percent down payment with current raisable rents. Full price $720,000.

Clyde Realty   **476-8200**

The above heading gives the number of units and their location. Raisable rents and positive cash flow are strong plus points.

Fixer-Upper—4BR

An unpleasant odor permeates this brick Traditional in lovely Westport. You'll probably discover the source when you clean up the debris, but please don't tell us. We recommend that clean-up of the 8 rooms, basement and double garage start with a shovel and dump truck. This is not for the faint of heart or persons with a weak back, but a bargain is possible at $79,500.

Clyde Realty   **476-8200**

The two important features of this home are found in the simple, but effective heading.

Westlake

You can own a like-new, 3BR, 2½-bath Tennessee Colonial with all the fine detailing and craftsmanship you thought had been forgotten. A 2½-car garage, central air, a family room and a prestigious

WESTLAKE

address are yours for just $187,500.

Clyde Realty   **476-8200**

You can call attention to location by using a split heading, which is effective for a highly desirable area.

$150 Per Month

is your total rent in this quiet family park in Westwood. The 24' × 60' home features 2 full baths, a family room and 2 oversized bedrooms. It comes with all appliances, some furnishings and great financing at $29,500.

Clyde Realty   **476-8200**

FIGURE 4.3   Feature-Oriented Classified Ads (continued)

Tall Trees

create a screen of privacy, and soft cascades of light and shade add a timelessness where today, tomorrow or next week need not mean urgency. In this very special place stands a home as solid as the trees that guard it. This 3BR, 2-bath American Traditional has an unassuming charm that complements the environment. Four acres of a very special love priced at $179,500.

Clyde Realty   476-8200

This ad is for an older home on a wooded parcel, and it effectively sells a mood.

The ad was taken with permission from an award-winning ad written by Gordon Wearing-Smith for Barry Plant Real Estate, Doncaster, Australia.

$69,500—4BR

We are serious. This redbrick American Traditional is really available. It is located in an established North Side neighborhood where owners take pride in their homes. Only a short walk to schools and parks, this home has a full basement, garage and a delightful garden spot. Best of all, it qualifies for

No-Down/Low-Down

VA or FHA financing. Please believe us when we say "You should call now, as this opportunity will not last."

Clyde Realty   476-8200

The home's strong features—its price and size—are combined for the first heading. The second heading sells the terms available.

Walk to University

This is an exceptional 3-bedroom, brick bungalow located on a quiet street with a separate, paneled dining room; a living room built for entertaining; a picturesque front porch; and rose bushes that are the pride of the neighborhood. By renting 1 or 2 rooms to students, your payments can be practically made for you. It's an unusual opportunity at $89,500, with great terms.

Clyde Realty   476-8200

This ad stresses the benefit of living close to a university. It will appeal to people other than just students and employees because of its income possibilities.

Middleton

with its quiet, tree-lined streets and old values, is the site of this 3-bedroom American Traditional that appears to be right out of a Norman Rockwell painting. Your children will love the softball-sized backyard with room to spare for a garden. There is plenty of room to tinker in the oversized garage and the basement makes a great rainy-day playroom. Invest in your family today at $98,000.

Clyde Realty   476-8200

The heading sells location, while much of the ad body sells the picture of an ideal family environment.

FIGURE 4.4 Intriguing Classified Ads

If It Ain't Broken

don't fix it. This 3BR, 1½-bath Cape Cod in Weston Heights is perfect the way it is. It has landscaping to turn your friends green with envy; new Berber carpeting; drapes in soft, neutral tones; a fully finished basement ready for your hobbies, entertaining or as a fitness center; and a great deal more. It's ready for you at $89,500.

Clyde Realty   **476-8200**

The Collie Next Door

hopes the new owners of this 3BR, 1½-bath, split-level in Washington Heights have a friendly dog to share her trees with and to gossip through the back fence. By the way, besides a fully fenced yard the home offers several large trees of its own, a lovely flower garden (perfect for burying bones), a double garage, a fireplace to cuddle up by, a large family room for romping and a country kitchen with the biggest refrigerator you ever saw (perfect for storing bones). The friendly owner priced it at $87,500, so pick up the phone and give a "whoof" to

Clyde Realty   **476-8200**

THIMK!

and you will realize this 3BR, 2-bath Cape Cod with a 2-car garage on a wooded lot in Westhaven is a fantastic opportunity at $89,500.

Clyde Realty   **476-8200**

The intentional misspelling in the heading will be pointed out by callers.

Leave It to Beaver

Hey! His home and neighborhood really do exist, and they can be yours. You'll love this 3BR, 1¾-bath, two-story, white clapboard Colonial with its wide, covered porch; picket fence; and quiet tree-canopied street. It's as if a whole neighborhood was taken from the past and lovingly preserved for your future. This is definitely a *must see* at $89,500.

Clyde Realty   **476-8200**

This ad mostly sells image. Very little is said about the house itself. The purpose of the ad is to whet the reader's appetite for more information.

Doctors' Row

A block party in this Pinewood Cove community will seem like a medical convention. This 3BR, 2½-bath English Tudor estate is the perfect home for a hypochondriac. When not providing the neighbors with your symptoms, there's a heated pool and spa for therapy and a fantastic garden guaranteed to lower your blood pressure. This home has all you expect and more with its fine French doors; leaded-crystal, cut windows; exquisite woodwork; a kitchen that will make you want to eat at home; and a richly paneled library. Hurry, or a doctor will beat you to it at $469,500.

Clyde Realty   **476-8200**

This ad treats the home's quality neighbors in a very light manner.

FIGURE 4.4 Intriguing Classified Ads (continued)

One-Legged Alligator Hunter

has decided to sell this 3BR, 2-bath waterfront home on beautiful Lake Louise. There's a gentle sand beach where fishing from the dock is reported to be great! You'll love the fully screened Florida room, where you can sit and enjoy the sunset. For weekends, weeks on end or a lifetime, this can be your very special place. Specially priced for you at $119,500.

Clyde Realty   **476-8200**

The heading is, of course, a spoof to get the reader's attention. Because "waterfront" is a prime feature, this heading should only be used when the ad is under a waterfront category in the newspaper.

Who Used the Tub?

We suspect Mr. Buckley of our office has been bathing in the Italian marble tub in the sumptuous master bath of this 3BR, 2½-bath Italian Renaissance estate in Westhaven. Every afternoon he visits the house and takes along a towel. When he returns, he's singing Italian arias. When you see the tantalizing Roman baths, you'll want to join him. The estate has an aura of elegance that makes you want to pamper yourself. With more than 3,500 sq. ft. of sheer luxury and almost a half-acre of grounds, this is your chance to be good to yourself for $349,500. After all, who deserves it more?

Clyde Realty   **476-8200**

The above heading is a real attention getter.

A Goldfinch and a Hummingbird

were at the feeders when we visited this 3-bedroom, brick American Traditional on a large corner lot. The backyard is a delight with colorful plantings and a family vegetable garden. The house includes a 2-car garage, full basement, hardwood floors and best of all, you'll fall in love with the quiet, friendly neighborhood of well-kept homes and lawns. This is a great family or retirement home at only $77,500.

Clyde Realty   **476-8200**

Not much is said about what is probably a 1-bath, smaller, older home.

Ralph Washington Slept Here

It is reputed that Ralph, no relation to George, spent at least 1 night in this new, 3BR, 2-bath Colonial while it was under construction. Despite Ralph's brief occupancy, the home turned out extremely well. The wood floors and trim; used-brick fireplace with a mantle made from an ancient beam; and brick, copper and tile family kitchen all add a feeling of gentle warmth. You'll love the bay windows and the family room that opens onto your own wooded grove. Of course, all the amenities are present, such as air conditioning, a 2½-car garage, and a full basement awaiting your finishing touches. After Ralph, you can be the second person to sleep here for $197,500. This moment in history is brought to you by

Clyde Realty   **476-8200**

This ad is a takeoff on ads used by some brokers on historic homes.

FIGURE 4.4   Intriguing Classified Ads (continued)

Nobody Slept Here

unless it was Hank the plumber, who seems to have put in quite a few extra hours on the job. This 3BR, 2-bath Dutch Colonial in a quiet, village-like setting in New Glares offers solid hardwood floors; a full basement; an oversized double garage with automatic opener; a positively dream kitchen loaded with copper, tile and brick; a recreation room big enough for a family reunion; walk-in closets; and darn near everything you can think of. This home will have the Jones family trying to keep up with you. Don't tell them you only paid $249,500.

Clyde Realty   **476-8200**

$1,000,000

If you are one of the few who can get past the price, you'll want to know about this 3BR, 3½-bath, Italian Renaissance estate set on 2½ acres in Holiday Hills. You'll delight over the feeling of gracious spaciousness, the quality accouterments, the lovely rose garden and entertaining patio, the championship tennis court and the Olympic-sized pool. If you're one of the very few within reach of such a residence, call.

Clyde Realty   **476-8200**

The price is used in this ad to attract attention.

Are You a Leo?

If so, you are bored with the commonplace. At last we have a home as individual as you are, one that stands out from the sameness of tract homes. Designed by Royal Wilson in the Prairie style of Frank Lloyd Wright, this 3-bedroom, 2½-bath masterpiece offers a private den with its own entrance, a kitchen that puts those in *House and Garden* to shame, a 3-car garage and by far the finest estate site you can find, with massive oaks and stately maples. We are not "lion" when we say, "This is as good as it gets at $398,500."

Clyde Realty   **476-8200**

Mentioning an astrological sign in a heading will practically guarantee the ad will be read in its entirety by a great many people. Even nonbelievers read their horoscopes.

Mrs. Higgins Was Mortified

when she discovered that the last visitors to her 3BR, 2½-bath, double-garage Colonial had walked on the sparkling ceramic-tile floor and soft Berber carpeting with dirty shoes. She says that she won't sell her dream home to people like that. If you really want a home that surpasses everything you have seen, in an estate setting and for $187,500, then you better wipe your feet first.

Clyde Realty   **476-8200**

They Wouldn't Believe Me

when I told them we had a newer, 3BR, brick, 2-bath ranch home with double garage, central air, and room to park their RV on the West Side for only $89,500. Maybe I was lying, but just suppose I wasn't. Call Cliff Henderson at

Clyde Realty   **476-8200**

Note that this ad names a particular salesperson.

FIGURE 4.4   Intriguing Classified Ads (continued)

The British Are Coming

At last a proper British Town House! This redbrick, 3-bedroom, 2-bath residence reflects the subdued quality of fine craftsmanship. The proper English garden is enclosed by a high wall, and there's a garage for 2 motor cars. Offered to you at $93,500, it's strongly recommended you contact the estate agent at once.

Clyde Realty   **476-8200**

A Dozen Kids A Billiard Table A Mean Mother-in-law

would all fit into this 11-room, 2-bath American Traditional set on almost a full acre in Westwood. There's even a full basement that will make a great workroom or dungeon, depending on your interests, and a large garage. Best part is the price—only $117,500.

Clyde Realty   **476-8200**

This ad is for a large, older home. It was inspired by Ian Price of Surfer's Paradise, Australia.

Fire the Landlord

Own a 9-room, 3BR home for only $47,500 with payments less than the rent for a small apartment. With just $2,000 down, it's your opportunity to build equity, not save rent receipts. Call today, and give your notice tomorrow.

Clyde Realty   **476-8200**

Very little is said about the above home. This ad sells price and terms and is designed to make your phone ring.

Ringo Starr

didn't stay here, but Beatle records were played constantly in the separate teen suite of this 3BR, 3-bath Colonial with 2½-car garage in the nicest area of Orchard Heights. The basement recreation room can hold more than 100 screaming teenagers. The owners maintained their sanity because of the split floor plan. They also used the backyard garden as their escape. Their children are now grown, so it's your turn at $179,500.

Clyde Realty   **476-8200**

Like To Sit

and watch your neighbors run, jog and bike? The covered front porch of this 3BR, 2½-bath Victorian-inspired masterpiece is just the spot for watching. Shaded by giant beech and maples, this is indeed a tranquil spot. The wide, quiet, tree-lined street seems to act as a magnet to exercise freaks. Be strong, or you could be drawn into the madness. All yours at a lazy $189,500.

Clyde Realty   **476-8200**

"Victorian-inspired" means it is of fairly recent vintage but built in the Victorian architectural style.

FIGURE 4.4   Intriguing Classified Ads (continued)

A Curious Raccoon

watched as we put up the For Sale sign on this 3BR, 2-bath sprawling brick ranch home just 20 minutes from the city. The home features big-city conveniences; large, bright rooms; central air; a quiet den; and a rose brick fireplace with the added charm of rural America. Your children will love the miles of trails, trees, wild animals and friendly neighbors (both 2- and 4-legged). Set on 3 acres all your own, this is the chance to make all your labors worthwhile. $187,500.

Clyde Realty   **476-8200**

Herman Didn't Know

that he could buy a 3-bedroom, brick home with garage on a large, landscaped lot in a choice West Side location for

$2,000 Down

and a full price of $56,000. That's why Herman is still renting.

Clyde Realty   **476-8200**

This unusual heading will attract the reader's attention.

Why Would They Sell

a 3BR, 2-bath, West Side ranch home with a double garage in almost model-home condition for thousands less than its replacement value? Frankly, we don't know the owner's motivation. The owner knows what we think it's worth but has, nevertheless, set the price at $129,500.

Clyde Realty   **476-8200**

Orthodox Druid

wishes to sell this 3-bedroom, West Side, Colonial Manor House so she can commune with nature. Actually, this home is in like-new condition, as I think the owner spent most of her time tending her magnificent flower, vegetable and herb gardens. There's a delightful conservatory perfect for an artist's studio. If you buy the house, don't cut down the big oak in the front yard, as the owner indicated that it's her great grandfather. Priced to send the owner away quickly at $189,500.

Clyde Realty   **476-8200**

This ad will attract attention and much discussion, but make sure you have an owner with a slightly twisted sense of humor who agrees to the ad.

Arrowheads and Pottery Shards

have been reported found on this 10-acre, mostly wooded site, which is only 45 minutes from the civic center. While the Indians who lived here didn't commute, they must have enjoyed the clean, crisp air; the chatter of squirrels in the hickory trees; magnificent vistas; and cold, clean water flowing year-round from a natural spring. The old ways are surely the good ways, and they can be yours at $79,900.

Clyde Realty   **476-8200**

This ad appeals to people looking for a homesite. Indian artifacts are a very positive feature for many buyers.

Source: *Simplified Classifieds—1001 Real Estate Ads That Sell.* Copyright 1990, Dearborn Financial Publishing, Inc., Chicago.

FIGURE 4.5 Nostalgia-Based Classified Ads

Remember Kick the Can?

There's still a place where children can run free and neighbors still sit on front porches on warm summer evenings. This 3-bedroom Nantucket Colonial offers more than just the charm of a gentler time. It also offers your family the way of life they deserve at an affordable $97,500.

Clyde Realty   **476-8200**

This ad sells nostalgia. It causes the reader to think back to the pleasant aspects of his or her childhood and makes an older home seem very desirable.

Dixie

Young men sang as they marched down a tree-canopied lane past this then-new 3BR, white-clapboard home. The owners waved the flag with the stars and bars from their rocking-chair front porch. While there have been many changes since that time, the home still stands amidst flowering shrubs and magnolia trees as lovely as long ago. It has been skillfully updated to provide all modern conveniences without sacrificing any of its charm. Available for your family at $79,500.

Clyde Realty   **476-8200**

When advertising a northern home, consider "Battle Hymn of the Republic" as the heading.

Fiddler on the Roof

This house has tradition. Built in 1870, this 8-room, 3-bedroom Edwardian masterpiece has seen America grow from the days of horse-drawn carriages to modern times. It has been home to suffragettes and Civil War veterans. The long covered porch has heard tales of the days when the country was new, and the front parlor held many nervous young beaus who came courting. This happy home of the past has much happiness to give for your family's future. A rare bit of Americana can be yours for only $89,500.

Clyde Realty   **476-8200**

This ad sells a mood to make the home desirable.

Hopscotch

is still played on the sidewalks of this quiet, tree-lined street. You will hear the sound of roller skates and carefree laughter. This 3BR, 1½-bath Cape Cod, set back from the street behind a white board fence and colorful plantings, offers a full basement, hardwood floors, formal dining room, country kitchen and a basketball hoop on the double garage. Waiting for your family's tomorrow at an old-fashioned price—$87,500.

Clyde Realty   **476-8200**

FIGURE 4.5 Nostalgia-Based Classified Ads (continued)

Step Back 60 Years

You can live on a quiet street with huge maple and chestnut trees, large homes that show their owners' love and neighbors who care. You'll take a giant step back in time as the owner of this 3BR, white-clapboard Traditional with its tribe-sized kitchen, formal dining room, old-fashioned front parlor, high ceilings and bright sense of spaciousness. There's an old-fashioned garden with sweet peas and hollyhocks. Your escape from today at $79,500.

Clyde Realty   **476-8200**

A Call from the Past

Want to live in a quiet, friendly neighborhood with children roaming freely, old-fashioned front porches, pride in one's home and respect for one's neighbors? You can have it all today with this 3-bedroom American bungalow with its full basement, storage attic, garage and very special garden at a price truly old-fashioned, $69,500.

Clyde Realty   **476-8200**

Remember Grandmother's House

with the gleaming hardwood floors, rich wood paneling, corn-popping fireplace and old-fashioned bay window with a window box full of treasures? Well, it has been carefully preserved for you in this 3-bedroom American Traditional that combines the best of the past with modern conveniences of today. Don't look for reproductions when the real thing is available for only $89,500.

Clyde Realty   **476-8200**

1896

Civil War veterans led the July 4th parade, horsepower still referred to horses and a man's home was truly his castle when this turreted, 10-room Victorian, with its lavish wood trim and high ceilings, was built for gracious living. If you desire to recapture the joy of a gentler time, call today for a private showing. Offered at $179,500.

Clyde Realty   **476-8200**

The year an older home was built can make an effective heading. The ad body above creates a pleasant, nostalgic image.

Source: *Simplified Classifieds—1001 Real Estate Ads That Sell.* Copyright 1990, Dearborn Financial Publishing, Inc., Chicago.

Being Negative

Real estate ads are an exception to the general rule that negative ads do not work. In fact, you will find ads that actually denigrate property will receive exceptional response, the reason being the readers will practically taste the possibility of a bargain. In addition to fixer-upper ads, negative headings tell people not to do something. For some strange reason, readers will read ads with this type of heading. Of course, you will need

---

FIGURE 4.6 Negative Classified Ads

The Roof Leaks

the paint is peeling and the plumbing is not well in this 3-bedroom Cape Cod with double garage on a quiet, tree-lined, West Side street.

Fix It Up

and it can be the pride of the neighborhood instead of its shame. Priced to reflect problems at $79,500.

Clyde Realty   **476-8200**

A split heading is very effective. The positive features of this home are its basic structure (Cape Cod with double garage), location and price.

Only 1 Bedroom

That's right. The only guests you'll have better be mighty good friends. Designed for a couple, this miniature estate offers an expansive living area that looks out upon a private garden patio. There's also a dream kitchen with an illuminated ceiling and a large double garage. All the space you need at an affordable $79,500.

Clyde Realty   **476-8200**

This ad is for a single-family home, but it could also be used for a condominium.

4BR Nondescript

If it had any less class, we'd raise the price and call it a classic. There are 9 nondescript rooms in this rather nondescript brick residence located in one of the most desirable areas of Westhaven. "Unimpressive" is a word that fits the landscaping. It's the perfect home for the nondescript family at only $89,500.

Clyde Realty   **476-8200**

Are You Eccentric?

If so, you'll love this tasteless, 3BR, 2-bath West Side Colonial. While Miss Jones of our office thinks it's cute, one of our buyers described it as "early brothel" with the bright reds accented by pinks and mauve. The house looks great on the outside; apparently the decorator didn't get around to that yet. The house does have central air, a full basement, a 2-car garage and a beautiful natural stone fireplace. If you're color-blind, it's a fabulous find at $219,500.

Clyde Realty   **476-8200**

The decorating is the only problem with this home. It will attract fixer-upper buyers who can visualize how to improve the property.

The Bottom of the Barrel

We avoided advertising this one as long as possible, since it will take a miracle to sell it at any price. Sure it has 3 bedrooms, 2 baths and is in a desirable West Side neighborhood, but beyond this, there's nothing else that's positive. To say it has been neglected would be a compliment, as it needs just about everything. We know it's habitable because we found an old mattress and a pile of cigarette butts in a corner of the basement. The price is a low $59,000, but don't expect much.

Clyde Realty   **476-8200**

This ad will make the phones ring. It was inspired by a Roy Brooks ad (London, England).

FIGURE 4.6 Negative Classified Ads (continued)

Miserable

That's how Mrs. Hopkins of our office describes this 3BR, 2-bath newer Cape Cod in a rather fashionable West Side neighborhood. The decorating is early dungeon style (dark and dreary), the garden features weeds and thistles and the carpets are badly stained. There are some nice hardwood trees, a double garage and a rather nice family room with a fireplace, but frankly, right now the house does look depressing. The price is also depressed at $89,500.

Clyde Realty   476-8200

Note that the negative features of this home are really cosmetic in nature and are far outweighed by the positive features.

Don't Buy This Home

Mrs. Kelly of our office has fallen in love with this 3BR, 2-bath, Morningside Heights Colonial. She says this home has "an ambiance of happiness because of its brightness and spaciousness." (Mrs. Kelly talks this way.) The home has a double garage, family room, central air, greenhouse kitchen and 4 apple trees. Mrs. Kelly hopes no one looks at it until she talks Mr. Kelly into moving. At $189,500, she claims it's a real bargain, and she's a professional.

Clyde Realty   476-8200

This simple heading will practically force a reader to look at the entire ad. Its humor makes this ad stand out.

The Basement's Damp

We aren't sure if the leaking roof has anything to do with it. This brick 3BR Cape Cod in Dorchester has definitely seen better days. In its favor, there is a nice 2-car garage with a paved driveway and some beautiful trees sprinkled among the weeds and bare patches of ground. Because of unusual circumstances, this home has been vacant for over a year, so check it out carefully because with a price of just $49,500, there must be a lot more wrong with it.

Clyde Realty   476-8200

This ad will excite the true buyer of fixer-uppers.

Looks Like Old Money

is what your guests will say about this dingy monstrosity that skillfully blends the ugly with the vulgar. The 11 rooms on a rather tasteless street of similar residences (considered by many to be fashionable) show a patrician disdain for beauty in favor of gauche. It's the perfect home for the social climber who wants to appear to have arrived at $280,000.

Clyde Realty   476-8200

This ad is for a large, older home in an area of people with old money. It makes fun of buyers who want this type of home, although the ad will attract them.

FIGURE 4.7 Romantic Classified Ads and Sexual Double Entendres

Love in the Air

Twenty-two stories above the world is a 2BR, 2-bath private place made for you. There are two balconies—one ideal for dining and entertaining above the lights and the other for soaking in the sun. Rooms of generous proportions and amenities include a wood-burning fireplace, a state-of-the-art kitchen, jacuzzi baths sheathed in marble and an incomparable river view. An opportunity unlikely to be repeated at $389,500.

Clyde Realty   **476-8200**

A Fallen Woman

Once she was stately and acceptable by the best of society; today she stands empty and worn. This 9-room, 3BR, turreted Victorian in the desirable Newhall area offers limitless possibilities and a challenge to the bold. With the curved wraparound front porch, intricate detailing and hardwood floors, this can be a home that knows no equal. Control her destiny for $89,500.

Clyde Realty   **476-8200**

This ad is really for an older, fixer-upper home.

Do I Have the Girl for You

Of course she's a bit old-fashioned. I guess you would say she's Victorian. She will never see 30 again, or 60 or even 90. Nevertheless, she's as good as she ever was, standing like a bride in her new coat of white paint. She has classic lines with her gently curved, wraparound porch; twin turrets; and fine detailing. You could even say she's magnificent. Inside, she has been carefully updated yet retains all that is gracious. Her 10 rooms will suit even the largest family, and she has been known to entertain dozens at a time. This is a home you'll want to bring mother home to, available now at $187,500.

Clyde Realty   **476-8200**

While an allegorical ad such as this is difficult to write without being overly cute, this one comes off well, even with its feminine references.

Topless

Ceilings seem to soar forever in this 3BR, 2½-bath, Mediterranean Renaissance residence in Belwood Heights. Other amenities include a 3-car garage, magnificent fireplace sheathed in marble, Grecian tile, gallery dining room and everything on your wish list. Down-to-earth priced at $249,500.

Clyde Realty   **476-8200**

Undressed

This brand-new, 3BR, 2-bath, double-garage Colonial is awaiting your individual touch. There's still time to choose the colors. You'll love the high ceilings, authentic moldings and the feeling of bright spaciousness. Set on an estate-sized lot on the most desirable street, this is an opportunity that won't last long at $179,500.

Clyde Realty   **476-8200**

The above heading will ensure that the ad is read. A more racy heading would be "Undressed and Waiting."

Source: *Simplified Classifieds—1001 Real Estate Ads That Sell.* Copyright 1990, Dearborn Financial Publishing, Inc., Chicago.

FIGURE 4.8 Classified Ads for Luxury Homes

A Home You Deserve

You have worked hard for your family, and this 3BR, 3½-bath French Regency reflects your success. With its walnut-paneled den; leaded glass; French doors; 40-foot living room; and of course pool, spa and cabana, this is the ultimate in material things life has to offer. An enviable estate at $1,200,000.

Clyde Realty **476-8200**

Palatial Estate

This turreted French Norman estate offers a charismatic blending of regal splendor and delicate charm. Fourteen magnificently proportioned rooms resplendent with elaborate details provide the epitome of elegant living with all the amenities one would demand of a home of this stature. Set amid lush, landscaped grounds bound to be envied, this estate may be copied but will never be equaled. It's the ultimate statement of your success at $2,900,000.

Clyde Realty **476-8200**

This ad really tells very little about the house other than that it is large and of high quality.

To the Manor Born

This proper English residence is a product of the golden age of architecture when cost ran a distant second to beauty. Set on an estate lot in Westbury Heights, the home offers 3 bedrooms, 2½ baths, a paneled estate office, a baronial-sized dining room and so much more. The home clearly shows the love craftsmen had for their art. This is a home as distinctive as yourself set amidst landscaping second only to Hampton Gardens. It's offered for your family and your family's family at $439,000.

Clyde Realty **476-8200**

This heading was, of course, the title of an English television series that was set on a fine English estate.

Superlatives Fail Us

We could use words like "magnificent in concept and proportion," "a world-class residence," and "a home to be envied," but words alone don't do justice to this exceptional residence. If you're one of the very fortunate few, we offer everything on your wish list at $1,650,000. Call today for a private showing of the indescribable.

Clyde Realty **476-8200**

The price limits calls to qualified buyers. The fact that absolutely nothing is said about the house will entice readers.

FIGURE 4.8   Classified Ads for Luxury Homes (continued)

Reflect Your Success

Don't you deserve a home that mirrors your achievements? This brick and stone English Regency on an estate setting in Woodridge Heights combines architecture and craftsmanship into a home that whispers, "success." With its high ceilings, massive beams and gleaming hardwoods, this spacious 3BR and den, 2½-bath home provides over 3,000 sq. ft. for gracious living. You'll love the rock-scaped pool, your own championship tennis court and the impeccably maintained grounds that provide an ambiance of quality living. For a very special few at $890,000.

Clyde Realty   476-8200

Life Is Full of Compromises

but you need compromise no more. This 10-room, Italian Renaissance residence has been thoughtfully planned to provide the ultimate lifestyle for those accustomed to the very best. From the magnificent public rooms to Roman baths sheathed in marble and the library with its solid walnut wainscoting, you'll immediately appreciate the superior appointments. Set on breathtaking grounds, the description "magnificent" seems like an understatement. Proudly offered to the very few at $870,000.

Clyde Realty   476-8200

Cloistered

Set among giant oaks in an exclusive community of fine estates, this 3BR and den, 2-bath French Regency offers a double garage, family room and central air. The understated elegance seems to whisper, "quality." Offered to the family accustomed to the very best at $249,500.

Clyde Realty   476-8200

This ad has an unusual heading to pique the interest of readers. It is for a better-quality, family home. Very little is said about the home—hopefully just enough to prompt a telephone call.

World-Class Residence

Once in a rare while will a truly magnificent home such as this be available. Built without compromise, the home reflects only the very best. This 17-room American classic has baths sheathed in Grecian marble; woodwork of American walnut; leaded-crystal, glass windows; a slate roof; and all the amenities present on your wish list including a lighted championship tennis court and heated Olympic pool. Set on 12 rolling acres, it is what success is all about. If you promised yourself the best in life, you can keep that promise at $2,600,000.

Clyde Realty   476-8200

Source: *Simplified Classifieds—1001 Real Estate Ads That Sell.* Copyright 1990, Dearborn Financial Publishing, Inc., Chicago.

an owner with a sense of humor to use this technique. Be sure to discuss your strategy with the owner before running negative advertising. Figure 4.6 presents examples of negative ads.

Romance

A romantic or even a mild sexual double entendre can be effectively used in the heading to draw attention to the ad. However, care must be exercised. Crude or vulgar references could result in a strong negative reader reaction to your firm. The ads in figure 4.7 are effective in this use.

Self-Esteem

The need for self-esteem is the desire for prestige, for respect. Ads for luxury homes can appeal to this powerful need (figure 4.8).

Note the use of adjectives in the ads to *paint* the desired image. You can write your own classified ads to rank with the best but it takes time and effort. *Classified Secrets—Writing Real Estate Ads That Work* (Real Estate Education Company) is an invaluable tool to assist you in writing ads. For those who don't have time to be creative *Simplified Classifieds—1001 Real Estate Ads That Sell* (Real Estate Education Company) is organized by category, and is indexed to help you find and readily modify ads or parts of ads to meet your needs.

If you're good, expect your ads to be copied by competitors. Great headings and descriptive phrases lose effectiveness when you are just one of many advertisers using them. Regularly change ad headings and wording to avoid that shopworn appearance. Also avoid manipulating word placement in ads, such as in figure 4.9, as they are difficult to read.

FIGURE 4.9   Irregular Word Placement in Classifieds Makes Comprehension Difficult

---

Buy
This New

3BR, 2 Bath Colonial
In Weston Heights. You
will love it at only
$137,500

Clyde Realty
555-8200

PLANNING DISPLAY ADS

Generally, ads in sections other than the classified ads are regarded as display ads. Display ads are often larger than one column in width and often include illustrations or photographs.

Unless you have great photographs, line drawings may be your best choice. Line drawings or sketches are often made by tracing from a photograph. The advantage of line drawings is that they remain clear even when reduced in size or printed on poor quality paper.

Cost for display ads is affected by where it is placed within the paper. As an example, a back page ad in a paper will cost significantly more than an interior placement. Sunday ads cost considerably more than weekday ads because of greater circulation for Sunday editions.

If you take advantage of the "run of paper" (ROP) rate, you will pay a lower rate, but your ad could be anywhere in the paper. You should generally avoid an ROP rate. You at least want your ad in the real estate section.

Ads in weekday editions generally cost the same regardless of the day of the week. Some advertisers want to advertise the day the newspapers include food chain ads and coupons (often Wednesday or Thursday) because of the significantly greater circulation on these days at bargain advertising rates. We feel this is a false economy for real estate advertisements as the readers of these issues, which do not include real estate sections, are not looking for display ads of real estate developments. It is best to place real estate display advertising the day or days the paper includes real estate sections—usually Sunday editions and in some areas, Saturday editions.

Special editions of newspapers such as anniversary or special-event issues often have specific rates for their supplements. Keep in mind that, while these editions charge higher rates due to greater circulation, much of the increased circulation you pay for will be outside your market area. The only special supplements you should even consider would be those dealing with real estate that are read by homebuyers.

Combination rates are possible for several newspapers printed by and under the ownership of the same company. One problem with combination rates is you are buying some cross-readership, although repetition does help. The other problem is much of the ad coverage may be outside your market area.

Contracts are available for display ads. This obligates you to a number of column inches at lower rates for longer contracts and greater space minimums. The same considerations apply to display advertising as to classified ads.

FIGURE 4.10   "Killer Ads"

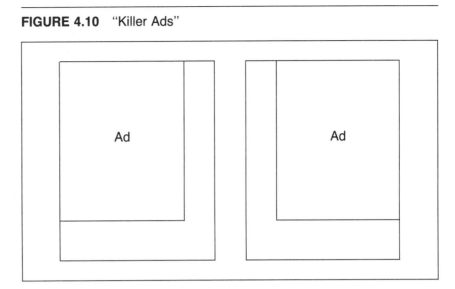

DISPLAY AD DESIGN

Special techniques can give your ads advantages. "Killer ads" or junior page ads, are less than one full page (often about two-thirds of a page) and have almost the effectiveness of a full page ad because they really "kill" the rest of the page (figure 4.10). In some cases, they can be more effective than a full-page ad, as articles continued from the first pages will usually be used to fill in the balance of the page, forcing readers to turn to that page.

Another kind of attention-getting ad is a "flex-form ad," which is usually L-shaped (figure 4.11). If used with a heavy border, such an ad will seem to jump off the page into the reader's eyes. Flex-form ads have greater effectiveness if used with a picture that conforms to the ad shape. The flex-form ad must have breaks based on the newspaper column width; even then, some newspapers will refuse them because they slow down the composition process.

In buying display advertising, you should realize type height is the measure in *points*: one point is $\frac{1}{72}$nd of an inch. A *pica* is used to determine column depth and width: each pica equals $\frac{1}{6}$th of an inch. The term *agate line* is $\frac{1}{14}$th of an inch in height by one column in width. Column width will vary among papers. Therefore, a column inch is not a set measurement, it is one inch in height by the width used by the newspaper for its columns.

Keep in mind that most real estate firms and developments predominantly market products to a local market. Ads in national, regional and even some large metropolitan area daily

FIGURE 4.11   Flex-Form Ad

Hillside Estates

New 3BR, 2 bath, split-level features family room, soaring entry, music loft, air-conditioning, double garage and every built-in imaginable for only $149,500.

Clyde Realty   555-8200

papers provide ad coverage beyond your market area, so a low cost per reader advertising rate is not necessarily a bargain.

Consider professional help in designing display ads. Your investment may be too great to risk to your intuition.

Here are a few basic rules:

- Most people read ads from the upper left-hand corner to the lower right-hand corner. When viewing a full-page ad, these readers would first see a headline across the top, followed by illustrations and copy in the center and ending with the firm name in the lower right quarter.
- One large picture is generally more effective than several smaller pictures.
- If reproduced well, photos may be more effective than drawings; in general, however, photos must be professionally retouched for reproduction. Retouching removes blemishes, increases contrast and can blur distracting backgrounds. Many photos used in ads are not retouched and sales suffer for it. In newspapers, a small photo will likely reproduce poorly because of poor printing and paper quality; therefore, with smaller ads drawings are usually better.
- Include white space. White space serves the purpose of emphasizing your message. It also isolates your message from those of competing ads. Trying to fill all your space can leave a cluttered ad that fails to attract readers.
- Don't use more than two type faces in an ad, as it detracts from its effectiveness. You generally have no control over the typeface style used for classified ads; however, hundreds of type styles are usually available for display ads, since you are supplying the camera-ready copy. Some advertisers choose a type style that is a little different than the type used by

others in the area. This adds a distinctive element to their ads. However, care must be taken so the type chosen doesn't detract from readability. Another problem with a distinctive type style is the possible adoption of this style by a competitor. It would eliminate your recognition factor and could even lead readers to contact a competitor after reading your ad.

- Ads on the top half of the page will generally generate more calls than do ads on the bottom half.
- Ads on the outside columns of the page will generally receive greater reader attention than ads on the inside columns. Unfortunately, some newspapers do not let you designate ad placement on the page or offer a guaranteed placement at a higher advertising rate. If you can get guaranteed placement and place display ads for different properties in that spot on the same day of the week, you will develop a following. People looking for homes will actually look to that spot for your ad.
- Type faces with serifs (tails) are generally more readable than type faces without tails (san serif).
- Avoid decorative type faces. They reduce readability and diminish the ability to capture the viewer at a glance. An exception would be the classic, simply styled word *Auction* to attract attention.
- Lowercase letters make for easier reading than capitalized letters.
- Short sentences are more readable than long sentences.
- Short words are better than long words, as they increase readability. Some experts say copywriters should strive to keep 75 percent of words used to five letters or fewer. Nevertheless, don't change a descriptive word for a shorter one if the shorter word is not effective in conveying the desired image.
- Ask for proofs (if you did not supply camera-ready copy) and review ads and proofs prior to submission. Make sure the ad is printed as proofed where and when it was to be printed. Minor errors can reduce ad effectiveness. Because of the large investment you place when advertising, notify the paper immediately about errors as well as to convey your expectations. Remedies could be to rerun the ad as corrected, or full or partial credit for the ad.

  Even when you supply camera-ready copy, some newspapers and magazines will reduce the ad size, put a border around it or both. If you don't want the ad reduced or otherwise altered, clearly state this in writing with your ad submissions.
- If you don't get the reader's interest in the first three lines of your ad, your reader is unlikely to continue reading. Therefore, you must command the reader's attention. Once

you have captured the reader, the reader is likely to continue. Readers will read long copy if you have captured their interest.

- Be mindful of the language level. Don't use words that might not be readily understood. Most people have several vocabulary levels. A good rule is if you wouldn't ordinarily use a word when talking to your family, don't use it in an ad. Novice ad writers tend to strain the limits of their vocabulary when writing ads. Remember that to sell, the ad must be understood. If the average ninth-grader wouldn't understand a word, don't use it.
- Don't be too subtle or sophisticated. Some copywriters get so clever they lose sight of their message and the readers.
- Always tell the reader where to obtain what you are offering (name, telephone number, and location).
- Always carry the same logo on your display ads as used for all your firm's signs, cards, stationery and if possible even your classified ads. You want to come across as one impressive firm, not a number of smaller ones.

If you prepare your own display ads, although we generally don't recommend it, a number of syndicated clip-art services can provide adequate artwork. Many clip-art books contain artwork specific to real estate. With your computer and computer clip-art, it is relatively easy to produce attractive copy with a laser printer.

The purpose of clip-art is strictly to gain attention. It does not help the selling process. A generic drawing of a house is not a substitute for a photograph or line drawing of the house you wish to sell.

WRITING COPY

Being a good ad writer isn't enough to turn out quality ad copy. It takes time and effort. You can, however, find a great deal of personal satisfaction in writing quality ad copy. You want your ad to be the best it can be, as your ad is in direct competition with those of your competitors for the viewer's interest. In these days of franchises and mega offices, the smaller your firm is, the better your advertising should be if your office is not only to grow but to continue to exist.

Your local paper probably offers ad preparation services. They may have excellent artists available (or clip-art libraries) and also good copywriters. Generally, the best you can hope for from your newspaper would be a slightly better-than-average ad. You are unlikely to get a great ad. The reason is basic economics: Newspaper staffs don't have the time to spend to make an ad great. Because they are paid relatively low wages, the copywriters and art directors are probably either fairly inexperienced or average at best. One frequent mistake of newspapers is to use identical clip art for ads from different firms. This reduces the image of uniqueness you want an ad to convey. You are not selling generic merchandise.

Like any other advertising, your ad must get the reader's attention, create interest, stimulate desire and result in action. If it does not inspire action your ad simply promotes your company.

You have a duty to your readers to provide truth, information and readability. Keep these duties in mind. Deceit may be used and even expected in an automobile advertisement, but you should strive to convey professionalism and integrity in your ads. Avoid any hint of deceit, even if others are doing it. As an example, some developers advertise prices for new homes with an asterisk (*). On the bottom of the page, which only an eagle could read, you find "*plus lot." This is simple deceit and will not bring your firm any goodwill.

Avoid special-effect photos that make a home appear larger than it actually is. The same holds true for artistic work. While adding landscaping to show how it could look is acceptable, changing the size is pure deception.

The quality of advertising copy varies inversely with the number of people who contribute to or edit ad copy. It is an illustration of the old adage, "An elephant is a mouse designed by a committee." While decision by consensus might work in some areas, in advertising it is usually fatal to the ad's effectiveness.

Reading the paper was once considered a significant portion of morning and/or evening activity. The average newspaper purchaser now spends about 15 minutes with it instead of an hour or hours as in the days before television. Because of this shortened exposure period, your ads must be better than ever to catch the reader's attention. Ads once read in their entirety by significant numbers of readers will now only receive cursory treatment unless your ad is able to grab the reader.

Writing good copy is a craft that can be learned. However, writing truly great copy is an artform that takes much more than technical knowledge. It takes both effort and creativity—it is the product of perspiration and inspiration.

In a good display ad, the general appearance must be attractive. Many viewers will pass over ads that are not attractive. Beauty may be only skin-deep, but your ad must have that beauty to get buyers through the door.

In preparing an ad, first write down the message you wish to convey in a concise manner. Now consider a heading that will entice a likely buyer to read your message. It can be a desirable feature or an attention-grabbing heading. Add adjectives to increase desirability. Now ask yourself, "Is there any part of this ad not likely to affect decision-making?" If there is, eliminate it. Now consider illustrations or photos that will help you sell the property. You now have a basic ad, which, except for some fine-tuning, is ready for the newspapers. Fine-tuning will consist of organization and word changes so the completed ad flows naturally and attracts attention, creates interest and motivates readers to act.

Before submitting the ad, ask yourself, "How large must the ad be to adequately state my message?" To limit your ad to a predetermined size because of cost can reduce the ad's effectiveness. The size should fit the ad, not the other way around.

TIPS OF THE TRADE

The specific techniques to use when writing ads are limited only by your imagination. Here are a few ideas to stimulate your own thoughts:

- *Understatement.* For example, an ad picturing a fine estate home could have copy such as, "An unassuming, proper residence." British ads frequently take this approach.
- *Emotion.* This can be very effective. Emotion plays an important role in home sales.
- *Testimonials.* What others are doing, and why, affects readers. Millions of dollars are paid to celebrities for endorsements because people are influenced by others. If the reader can relate to the person making the testimonial, the ad's message will be strengthened. A valid spokesperson could be another retiree or young professional family. If you extol the person or profession, the endorsement gains strength.
- *Color.* Color is not a requirement if your competitors are using it in display ads, as your use of color would not catch the reader's attention. However, if your competition does not use color, your use of color would make your ad far more effective. If the newspaper uses color on the front page of the real estate section, you should be able to get a good rate for a color ad on the back page, since that sheet must go through a press set-up for the color process. Custom spot color is expensive because it involves separations and separate printing plates.

  Color renderings are generally made from the plans before a building is constructed. They are usually watercolor portrayals of how the building will look when completed and landscaped. They are often made for a planning commission's approval or for an owner's use. Because renderings have a mystic quality, they can be used effectively in display advertising. They can also be used in brochures, property briefs, and even in press releases. To find artists who specialize in color renderings, consult any architect in your area.

- *Mistake*. A misspelled word or a line upside-down for no reason can work to your advantage. Peoples' eyes often focus on mistakes and they delight in telling others how the advertiser goofed. One broker held an "Open Housk" and reported an exceptionally good turnout, with several people telling him how the newspaper messed up his ad.
- *Classified ads*. A simple classified ad can become a display ad simply by blowing the ad up to a two- or three-column width. It will stand out like a sore thumb among the other display ads and, if it has an attention-getting heading, will be read (see figure 4.12).
- *Cute*. Avoid cuteness for cuteness' sake. While baskets of kittens or puppies are nice, they don't convey product or firm identification to the reader.

One broker used an unusual twist in her display ads during a period when buyers outnumbered the available properties. Each ad featured a family. One ad had the family standing in a wooded setting with props for the children (a girl holding a doll and a young boy holding the handle of his coaster wagon); even the family dog was in the portrait. The ad heading was:

**Wanted:
A Home for This Family**

The body of the ad then went on to tell about the family and their needs. The "wanted" ad campaign was highly effective in bringing in owners; the broker credited it with making her office one of the hottest in the area.

OUTSIDE HELP

Assume you have arrived at the moment of truth. You realize the ads you write are mediocre and your local newspaper isn't any better. You need help. While professional help should be considered if feasible (see the *"Advertising Agencies"* section in Chapter 1), there is still one more alternative: to take inspiration from the ads of others. Don't copy ads. What you should be looking for are ideas and approaches. Obtain Sunday editions

FIGURE 4.12   "Classified" Display Ad

Are You an Aries?

If so, you get what you want, and you want to be indulged by the best. This 3-bedroom, 2½-bath Colonial on the most desirable street in Westlake will please even the most fastidious Aries with its 2+ +-car garage, majestic maple trees, native stone fireplace, richly paneled den and a country-sized kitchen that will delight any chef. For $179,500, it can be your sign for the future.

Clyde Realty   **476-8200**

Source: *Simplified Classifieds—1001 Real Estate Ads That Sell.* Copyright 1990, Dearborn Financial Publishing, Inc., Chicago.

of major newspapers from other cities (never use local papers). Go through the display ads. You will see some excellent and original approaches that could be modified for the property you are marketing and which would appear totally original in your area. Even this approach has problems. Some people wouldn't know a great ad if it fell on them, "stealing" ideas from poor ads, which is pretty sad. If this is the case with you, hire a professional.

Figure 4.13 offers some examples of display ads that we think are quite good:

FIGURE 4.13   Creative Display Ads

LIMITED EDITION OF 32 HOMES IN LOMA LINDA

If you want to live at Pasatiempo, you better get moving.

Why the rush?
Well, our first phase nearly sold out the day it opened and the second phase is off to a fast start as well.

What makes Pasatiempo so popular?
Lots of things! Our homes are designed for family living with huge family rooms, family-size kitchens and big back yards.

Our location is hard to beat. We're nestled at the base of the foothills, near a great community park and right in the heart of family-oriented Loma Linda.

Our value. Compare our spacious plans, our large lots, our luxurious features and our great prices. You'll find there's no comparison.

So what are you waiting for?

**4 & 5 Bedrooms
Up to 2,899 Square Feet**

Priced from the low $200,000's

25725 Hinckley Street
Loma Linda, CA 92354
(714) 799-8185

The sales office is open daily 11:00 a.m. to 6:00 p.m. except Wednesday and Thursday.

PACIFIC SCENE, INC.

FIGURE 4.13 Creative Display Ads (continued)

OUR GRAND OPENING IS REALLY A HOMECOMING.

We're welcoming you home to Springdale Village. Cross the threshold to a special way of life. Where innovative designs assure that you and your family will have room to live, to relax, to entertain.

Our multi-featured three and four bedroom plans offer such uncommon luxuries as air conditioning, custom oak cabinetry, ceramic tile entries and so much more.

Plus, full sized lots of 7,700 square feet or more mean there's room to roam, to garden, to pro-vide a place for your child's play.

So, please be our guest and see for yourself.
Springdale Village
Come see it.
Come share it.
You'll always be welcome!
Priced from $89,900

1516 W. Mesa Drive
Rialto (714) 355-7893

SPRINGDALE *village*

WDS
WDS Development, Inc.

Bringing imagination and innovation home.

Sales office open Friday through Tuesday, 10:00 a.m. to 5:00 p.m.

Source: Wesselink Advertising. Reprinted with permission.

5 Electronic Media

When most people think of electronic advertising media, they think of television and after a few minutes they might add radio. While these are the primary media available, you will shortly realize there are also other choices.

TELEVISION

Television is a growing medium for real estate advertising. It can be used effectively to promote your products and your firm. Television advertising advances your image in your community and is a definite plus when you're seeking to represent owners in the sale of their homes.

You are probably familiar with a local broker who is a "talking head." He or she has chosen television as an advertising medium and goes before the camera talking about properties or services of the firm, with the majority of the commercial time focused on the broker's head. The broker's friends will say how great he or she was; after all, what are friends for? Some people will recognize the broker from advertisements so he or she has become a celebrity. For all the good a talking-head ad produces, the broker would be significantly ahead by buying similar coverage on radio for far less money. A talking head reduces television to a purely audio medium. Television is visual, giving you the opportunity to show your product. Use it this way or don't use it at all.

The first step in a television commercial is the storyboard. A storyboard includes camera instructions and specifies who is speaking and what is said. Some storyboards prepared by advertising agencies resemble cartoon strips. In evaluating your storyboard, you will be able to determine if the ad fits into its designed time frame. A standard television commercial runs 15, 30 or 60 seconds. The longer the message, the more the cost for airtime. Also ask yourself whether the message will become more or less effective by lengthening or shortening the message.

Carefully review your storyboard to be certain the advertisement is what you want. It is more economical to pay for a new approach now than end up with an ineffective commercial. Keep in mind that the visual image should get your message across without the audio—you don't need a constant stream of dialogue.

The visual effects possible with television are limited only by budget restraints. As an example, an animated character logo might be great for firm identification, but the cost of such animation rules out most real estate advertisers.

Once you agree on the storyboard, the production firm will give you a price quote. You can get competitive quotes for a storyboard prepared by an advertising agency, but keep in mind you're buying artistic talent. Price should not be your sole criteria in making a decision on who will film the commercial. In the end, the lowest price might turn out to be the most costly. Depending on sets, special effects, actors, etc., television commercials could vary in cost from several hundred dollars to more than $10,000.

Your television ads should be filmed on videotape rather than film so you can immediately view the results. Adjustments can be made immediately at little or no additional cost.

Many television stations have commercial production capability. A great many seem to specialize in talking-head commercials, but some stations can turn out quality work. Your television station can also direct you to commercial production companies in your area. In creating your commercials, you will want to view samples of previous ads done by the people with whom you will be working.

Television can be effectively used in negative advertisements. As an example, a vacant commercial property or a fixer-upper can be shown with the approach, "What can we do with this . . . ?" Emphasizing the property's problems and asking viewers for solutions will excite fixer-upper buyers and innovative investors.

Testimonials are another effective advertising technique. A testimonial could include a family with young children and a pet outside their new home explaining why they moved to the development. Additional coverage could be of them inside the home utilizing its features, or working in the garden, using the recreational activities of the area, narrated with appropriate dialogue. Such a testimonial presents a positive image of the development. A testimonial with just a talking head and no visuals is ineffective.

A real-life situation with actors used to depict scenes is an excellent video approach. Such video presentations take talent to write and require more characters, and may prove to be quite expensive. Real-life situations could depict one friend telling another about the family's new home with filmed coverage matching the dialogue. An effective variation could be a child playing with a dog or cat while being interviewed as to how he or she likes living in _____.

Real-life situations are "slice-of-life" commercials. A slice of life can be added to sterile home shots by having a puppy walk on-camera, followed by a very small child who picks it up and walks off-camera. Adding a slice of life gives the viewer an impression of the benefits the home offers.

Humor can be used in slice-of-life advertising. Exaggeration is used in the following storyboard:

Audio	Visual
"Is this your children's play area?"	View of busy street traffic from 1930s, with traffic speeded up.
"Are these your children's friends?"	Shot of a group of leather jacketed "toughs" near a brick building.
"Are these your children's role models?"	Shot of several unsavory looking persons involved in some sort of transaction with a girl dressed in mini-skirt and boots, cigarette in hand, leaning against a wall.
"If so, it's time to consider Hoffman Estates where 3BR, 2 bath homes start at $79,500 with only 5 percent down.	View of homes, exterior, interior, recreational area. Printed on screen under view of homes: **Hoffman Estates Starting at $79,500 5% Down**
"Our models are open daily 8 A.M. to 4 P.M."	On-screen message change: **Hoffman Estates Models Open Daily 8 A.M.–4 P.M.**
"Follow the Hoffman Estates sign from the Bellwood Exit from Highway 74."	View of Bellwood exit sign on freeway. On-screen printing: **Hoffman Estates Bellwood Exit Highway 74**
"That's Hoffman Estates, Bellwood Exit Highway 74."	On-screen view of directional sign at the Bellwood Exit: **Follow the sign from Bellwood Exit on Highway 74.**

This one-minute commercial combines humor with a strong name and product identification. It also could be considered a story-line commercial, which is a drama format with off-screen narration.

A similar 30-second commercial could open with a shot of a family, with mother, dad, three to five children and grandmother and grandfather in a small kitchen, 1930's-style refrigerator, and rickety furniture. The voice-over could be, "feeling a bit crowded in the present apartment or home?" (to which the whole family nods affirmatively). Audio, the voice-over could continue with, "then move to . . .", showing family in a spacious living room of one of the furnished model homes, and so on.

A "vignette" is a fast-paced series of views. This format works well accompanied by a musical jingle for a development. Some other simple techniques are to move from a wide-angle shot and zoom in on a particular feature. You can also fade in and out with an overlapping effect, going from scene to scene.

Some TV special effects are easy. As an example, a camera could start with an empty room of a home; suddenly, the room could be fully furnished; next, people would quickly appear. The same effect can be done with an empty yard. A swing set would appear, then, children and puppies. This approach provides instant visualization of living in the home.

Some network and cable TV stations have regular shows that feature homes currently on the market. These shows are usually aired on Saturday and Sunday mornings to catch househunters before they begin their weekend house search. Generally, the shows feature views of a home with a voice-over describing features. These are excellent programs for promoting your inventory. Property selected must appear to be priced competitively or lower than other properties on the show. If your property appears to be a bargain, then the benefit of your advertising is primarily paid by other ads that make your property appear to have a price advantage. While the producers will usually arrange taping, you would be wise to hire someone to direct your sequence. You also might want actors ready to add a slice of life to the commercial. Your ad will then stand out from the sterile views of your competitors. You might check the excellent talent in the film or theatre arts departments at your local college.

Don't attempt to feed your ego by creating or appearing in all your ads. Unless you have the voice and demeanor a casting director would choose, you and any family members should stay out of the commercials. Grandparents may adore seeing their grandchildren on TV, but it doesn't sell homes and just might make your firm appear pathetic, which is probably not the image you want to convey.

Don't knock the competition. You must sell yourself as a professional before you sell your product. Many buyers are turned off by ads that deride the competition. Remember, real estate brokerage is founded on cooperation.

News programs and weather reports generally have a large audience for whom TV holds their primary attention. These time slots are considered premium and are priced accordingly.

You can find bargain rates with radio and TV stations. Many stations have special preemptive rates. When they have been unable to sell all their time slots, the station contracts unsold slots at a reduced rate; however, if someone also comes along willing to pay full-rate, you will be bumped. Don't use preemptive rate ads for open houses or your salesperson could end up lonely. A run-of-schedule rate is another bargain rate, but it offers you no control over when your ad will be run. It could end up as a commercial break during a late movie. Many television stations offer a special rate package covering an assortment of time slots. It allows the station to fill less desirable slots by including them with prime-time slots.

Your television station advertising salesperson might talk about rating points. Each rating point is one percent of the total number of households in the viewing area. The combined rating of a package of time slots is known as the gross rating points. Because some of the same people are tuned into the same station at the different time slots could mean gross rating points of 25 might only be reaching 10 percent of the households. Syndicated services provide reports on local station viewers at various times of the day. These reports can be more representative of the viewing audience than some salespersons' claims.

If other real estate firms are competing in your market area, try to schedule your ads so they are not so close to the other ads, so as not to dilute your ads' effectiveness. If a competitor has so many ads that they dominate the real estate advertising on a particular station avoid that station. Instead, choose a station where your ads will be unlikely to be sandwiched between ads of a competitor.

Cable Television

If you are considering advertising on television, you might want to give serious consideration to cable. Of the U.S. households that have televisions, the cable television industry claims that 57 percent subscribe to a cable service. In many markets this figure approaches 100 percent. Cable advertising can be cost-effective, because the cable viewing market is more likely to match your firm's market area than would the network station, which has a far greater reach. Some cable companies will offer an attractive initial contract to allow you to test the effectiveness of their stations. A good way to evaluate effectiveness is to advertise several properties or developments solely on cable.

Classified Cable Ads. In the early days of cable TV, its operators frequently assigned one channel as an electronic bulletin board to meet public service requirements. The channel featured soft music and printed messages. Later, cable operators were able to sell advertising on these channels. The ads, like the bulletin-board messages, are visual only, with a musical background. In our discussions with brokers and developers who use these bulletin boards, we found that advertisers are pleased with the results. One developer claimed his cable messages during the week are as effective as a half-page newspaper ad, and costs significantly less.

Many of these bulletin board messages are being replaced with classified ad channels or photo advertising channels. Recent improvements in technology allow pictures and voice commentary, as well as special effects to be readily set up for automated viewing. Ads for these stations can be prepared from written copy and a photo as the advertiser looks on. Cost for a 15-second ad repeated three to four times daily for one week can vary from $25 to $60, including the production of the ad. The system has worked so well that at least one independent cable operator has leased 3 channels for these classified ads. Viewers hear commentary while the firm name, telephone number and pictures of the property show on the screen. This innovative concept should prove to be effective for real estate.

RADIO

Radio is far from dead. It has made a great comeback after its projected demise with the advent of television. The high prices of radio stations hint at the tremendous advertising demand for radio. Everyone has at least one radio in their homes today, and it is a rarity if a car fails to come equipped with a sound system.

Radio and television advertising have less residual value than print ads. Radio listeners can't check what was announced and carefully study your ad offer. Most radio listeners are in the driver's seat daily and so have even less chance of writing down any ad information. In radio advertising, especially, you should convey your firm's name, its location and what you are offering.

The standard lengths of radio commercials are 15, 30 or 60 seconds. Because your message is short, try to concentrate on one theme at a time. Don't try to sell too much and don't talk too fast. A 60-second commercial should have no more than 150 words, or the ad will sound rushed. Mention your firm name more than once, and, if not a common name, spell it. Again, include your office location, and, of course, if you are selling a development, spell out the location and repeat it.

Humorous ad messages are the most difficult to write. The printed ad can be more subtle than those on radio. You must rely on outrageous humor. When strained or subtle humor fails, the results can really be tragic.

Keep your radio ad message simple and sell benefits. The shorter your ad, the more effective it must be. Short, effective ads are difficult to write. Unless your ad has unusually strong impact, you will need a full 60 seconds to promote property or properties. Confine your message to short sentences and don't try any words you wouldn't use in talking with a neighbor or friend. One reason for keeping your ad brief is that people can completely tune themselves out to most radio ads. As an example, you might have listened to 30 ads while driving to work today and not be able to name even three of those advertisers.

Because there are so many ads on radio, your radio commercial must be exceptional to have a strong impact. This is one place where average won't cut the mustard. Background music can increase emotional appeal of an ad, but it tends to blur your message making it easy for the listener to turn off your ad. Musical jingles must be catchy, feature the firm name and must be repeated on a regular basis. Keep in mind that musical jingles are institutional ads, giving your firm ready name identification. They are not created to obtain action. Radio jingles should be professionally written and produced, and make listeners remember your name and telephone number.

Radio advertising can create a visual picture in the listener's mind. Sound effects can help create that picture. As an example, birds singing in the background could help create a positive picture when describing a garden. When describing a backyard of a family home, the sound of children playing could help set a mental picture. In describing a pool, you could use the sounds of children and splashing. If you indicated that Fido would love the six large trees in the backyard, a friendly "woof, woof" in the background would help to set a positive picture in the listener's mind.

A demonstration technique that would be costly or impossible on TV can be done very easily on radio. As an example:

A   Ladies and gentlemen, today we are going to demonstrate the speed in which Clyde Realty markets homes. Our Clyde Realty sales associate will prove that Clyde Realty is faster than a speeding bullet. June Schmidt will leave point A, triggering a gun aimed at point A; she will rush to point B, erect a For Sale sign and return to point A, where she will catch the bullet between her teeth. Are you ready? Take 48.

[Bang]

A   All right, folks, get ready for take 49. Do we have another Clyde Realty sales associate?

As bizarre as this commercial is, it will be remembered. It is pure institutional advertising.

The Voice

One advantage of radio advertising is the spoken word can be more dramatic than the written word. The simplest radio commercial is one read by an announcer (live or on tape). Emphasis with the voice, its volume, pitch, speed, pauses and resonance can convey personal feelings. Voice can also effect believability; therefore, the voice of your announcer is very important. Walter Cronkite, for example, relays conviction in his voice—you know whatever he says must be true.

The use of a well-known personality with a distinctive voice will immediately get the listener's attention. Many celebrities make hundreds of local commercials. One problem with celebrity voices is the time it takes to obtain the commercial. Local radio stations can order celebrity commercials for you through agencies that handle this type of advertising. As your inventory is constantly in flux, you can't use the celebrity voice to advertise an individual property. However, you can get around the problem by preparing various introductions, which could be taped in advance. Here is an example:

"Hi! I'm _____, and I want to tell you about a really outstanding home currently available through Clyde Realty."

The celebrity voice could even end the ad with one of a number of taped closings:

"I suggest you get over to Clyde Realty at Third and Main across from the Night-n-Day Market right away, as this home won't last long."

While a distinctive accent can gain a listener's immediate attention, it must not detract from your message. Anyone who has seen a British movie knows the difficulty at times of understanding what is being said. An obviously phony accent will convey a negative image. A crisp, refined English accent can be very effective in selling high-priced homes. The accent should fit the narrative and go something like this: "A truly dignified residence featuring a three-car garage to house your motor cars."

Once you use an announcer with an accent, employ the same person for both radio and television advertisements to maintain firm identity—don't use different voices.

Announcers often do the majority of local ads on small radio stations, and in some cases even double as advertising salespeople for these stations. Two problems arise in using a station announcer for your ads. First, the announcer may not be that good. Second, your ad loses that special identity you could get using a different voice. The communications department (English or speech) of your local college might be able to recommend a student or faculty member who has a strong, distinctive voice. Don't do the commercials yourself or have some member of your family do them unless one of you has a professional-sounding voice.

Radio Ad Planning

Radio stations publish advertising rates. Just because the rates are printed on a card does not mean they are cast in stone. Deviation is possible, especially for small stations. Unsold time slots mean zero revenue for a station and can never be reclaimed. Therefore, radio stations are often willing to negotiate special rates for unsold slots. This allows you to evaluate the effectiveness of various advertising media and advertising approaches at bargain rates. You want to contract for at least one month with two or more ads per day to give them a fair trial.

In many larger market areas, it is not necessary to buy your advertising time through the stations. You can often get time at bargain rates through barter houses. The barter houses arrange with stations to trade various goods for advertising time. They then resell the time slots, generally at significant discounts from posted rates. Advertising agencies know who has barter time available and can often arrange purchases.

There are far more radio than television stations. This proliferation of broadcasters has led to a very segmented marketplace. You will find radio stations appealing to very diverse interest groups. In deciding on a station, consider the demographics of listeners at various times during the day. Stations will provide this information. Also consider the demographics of the likely buyer of a particular property or development.

Consider your market area in making your station selection. While AM carries further and is generally preferred for a semirural area, AM is susceptible to electronic interference. Large transmission lines can play havoc with reception. Because of their more limited range, FM stations are more likely to match an urban firm's market area.

As on TV, the time your radio ads will be aired is critical. You want Saturday and Sunday morning time slots for a weekend open house. A particular property ad would air best during office hours when you can field all calls. Late-night ads for such property would probably fail to keep the listener interested long enough to call the following day.

The prime-time radio slots are the morning driving time between 6:00 and 10:00 A.M. and the evening driver listening time between 3:00 and 7:00 P.M. Radio time costs relate directly to the listening audience. The better the listener time slot, the higher the advertising rate. Stations with good morning and evening rush-hour traffic reports and traffic helicopters are generally very desirable. Even those who are not yet on the road or are waiting for someone driving in traffic listen to these reports. Advertising agencies have experts who evaluate stations and time slots to fit the demographics of likely buyers and they even buy the time for you. Radio time slots are often sold Monday through Friday, with weekend time slots priced separately.

You should consider *flashing,* also known as *pulsing.* This is a technique of short bursts of intensive radio advertising followed by a much weaker market presence. As an example, a firm might have a dozen spots per day for ten days, followed by 20 days with only three spots per day. The effect of this flashing or pulsing of heavy coverage is to give the listener the impression that you have a dominant market presence. You can rotate your radio time slots horizontally. This can give a flashing effect. With horizontal rotation, you buy your time slots for a 30-day period, but use the majority of the slots on a single day such as Monday. The next month, you could rotate to Tuesday, and so on. Vertical rotation refers to changing the time of day for your slots.

Types of Ads

While radio use for real estate advertising is primarily for institutional advertising or when advertising a major subdivision, it can be effectively used to advertise particular homes. A good approach is to have a daily house that is advertised in the same time slots each day.

Clyde Realty presents [*drum roll*] today's best housing buy. Clyde Realty takes you to lovely Brentwood Village. This three-bedroom, two-and-a-half-bath Dutch Colonial features a separate family room, rose brick fireplace, gleaming hardwood floors, built-in everything including central air and an oversize, double garage. Sheltered by century-old maples, there is a delightful dining patio for those summer evenings. Truly a home to be envied. Because of unusual circumstances, it is presently available at $178,500. But call now. That's Clyde Realty at 555-8200. That's 555-8200. Clyde Realty is located at 2761 West Main across from the Day-n-Night Market.

This ad mentions Clyde Realty four times, the telephone number twice and the location of the Clyde Realty office. The drum roll and initial announcement get listeners' attention.

Advertising a daily special will actually have listeners checking the station every day to see what you're offering. If you use the "today's best home buy" approach, you could employ a 15-second teaser ad. You will probably find calls are coming in on the "teaser" before the real ad copy is run:

> In just ten minutes, Clyde Realty will tell you about today's best home buy. An outstanding three-bedroom Westside ranch priced under $100,000.

In radio as well as television, you can use a slice-of-life, or situational, ad. The following slice-of-life ad is staged like an old-time melodrama:

A   When we last left Mary, her landlord Sam Slime has just entered her apartment.

[melodramatic piano music]

SS   I'm turning this apartment into a condo. Out in the cold with you!

M   Oh! Whatever will become of me?

TH   I, Tom Hendricks, ace salesman for Clyde Realty, will save you. Clyde Realty has three-bedroom, two-bath ranch homes in Clifton Hills starting at less than $100,000, and Clifton Hills is right at the Midvale Exit from Highway 17.

M   I've been saved, I've been saved! Take me to my new home!

A   The good guys at Clyde Realty win again with Clifton Hills Estates at the Midvale Exit of Highway 17. Tune in tomorrow as Mary chooses her new drapes.

The ad above uses an exaggerated situation to obtain humor.

A take-off on the famous Joe Isuzu auto ads might use the following dialogue:

A   Would you believe Clyde Realty is selling three-bedroom, two-bath homes on one-quarter acre estate lots in Westlake starting at 49 cents each?

B   No! I wouldn't believe that.

A   Would you believe Clyde Realty offers these homes with no payments for 20 years?

B   No! I wouldn't believe that either.

A   How about that Clyde Realty has new three-bedroom two-bath homes with double garages and central air-

conditioning on one-quarter acre lots in Westlake starting at $89,500 with low down FHA and VA financing?

B   Now that I can believe!

A   Clyde Realty is located at First and Main across from
the Day-n-Night Market. Stop in or call—they're in the
book.

Here's a different approach to consider:

*[Announcer in a hushed voice—similar to
announcer during a key shot at a golf tournament]*

A   This is Scott Thomas speaking to you from Ridgecrest,
just off Highway 17 at the Midvale Exit. We are about
to launch the new Nantucket, a brick-and-frame Cape
Cod, built the way craftsmen build homes. Three huge
bedrooms, two full baths, double garage, full basement,
oak floors at a price of only $119,500, and this includes
a full one-quarter acre estate lot. Now the crowd is
hushed as Mrs. Bush brings back her arm and . . .

[Sound like bottle crashing]

[Crowd roars]

[In excited voice]

It's official! The new Nantucket home in Ridgecrest is
now available at only $119,500 with FHA and VA fi-
nancing available. Follow the signs from the Midvale
Exit off Highway 17 to Ridgecrest. Ridgecrest, your new
home.

A testimonial ad can be very effective. The announcer could
ask residents why they purchased in a particular development.
Some testimonial ads, such as the following, use subtle ro-
mance to promote rentals in apartment complexes:

[Young feminine voice]

Before I moved to Coventry Garden Apartments on Clover
Lane in Bellflower, I would come home after work, eat a TV
dinner and look at the walls, hoping someone would call.
Now, when I get home, it's tennis, swimming or a soak in
the hot tub with my friendly neighbors, followed by a relaxing evening in the clubhouse. Maybe I should barbecue
tonight on my very private balcony. It's great for sunbath-
ing too. My only problem now is that at Coventry Garden
Apartments there are just so many choices. For only $495 a
month you can join me. Just follow the signs from Newport
Exit at Highway 17 to Coventry Garden Apartments on

Clover Lane in Bellflower. Maybe I'll put something special on the barbie for you!

This ad could be readily adapted for television with views of an attractive young man or woman, or even a couple, enjoying the pleasures of Coventry Garden Apartments.

Testimonial ads by members of minority groups selling benefits of particular properties could serve as powerful institutional advertising. Such ads point out to minority groups that you favor their business and will meet their needs in a fair and proper manner. The testimonial ad of a person respected in the community adds a strong element of credibility to an ad. Similarly, a carpenter or other trade person involved in construction who purchased in a development would convey a quality image. A radio commercial (or other media campaign) could include testimonials from many trade people as to why they chose a particular development. The messages should emphasize quality and value.

The following is a testimonial by a real estate salesperson:

My name is Richard Hayes and I am a real estate salesperson. I am just one of seven real estate professionals who have already purchased homes for our families in Newport Village. We chose Newport Village because of the great location, just west of the Santa Rosa Freeway at the Admiralty Way exit, and the great Newport Village value. The home I chose for my family has three bedrooms, den, two-and-a-half baths, three-car garage and a huge fenced yard and just about everything I would want was included in the price. Oh! The price: My home sells for $169,500 with low down FHA financing. That's Newport Village, just west of the Santa Rosa Freeway at the Admiralty Way exit. Welcome, neighbor!

The following is an ad aimed at prospective buyers by selling the idea of ownership, not a particular property:

Would you love to own your home but feel you can't afford it? Do you feel trapped with monthly rental payments? Here at Clyde Realty, we have helped hundreds of families just like yours become homeowners instead of making their landlords happy. They are now building substantial equity in their homes. Call or stop by Clyde Realty today to arrange for a free, no-obligation financial consultation. We will analyze your needs and help you plan your future. With our many financing options, perhaps you can become a homeowner right now. That's Clyde Realty at 555-8200. Clyde Realty is located across from the Night-n-Day Market at 612 West Main Street.

The ad is aimed at the lower end of the market. You would need an inventory of homes where low down financing was possible to use this type of ad.

Radio can be used for obtaining listings as well as for sales:

Would you like a nicer home or to move to a different area? Perhaps your home no longer meets your needs or you're considering relocating for some other reason. Before you do anything, you should know what your present home is worth. You can do this with a simple phone call to Clyde Realty at 555-8200. Clyde Realty uses computer-generated data of recent sales to provide you with your own competitive market analysis, reflecting what your home is worth right now on today's market. Clyde Realty provides this market analysis of your home for you at absolutely no cost or obligation. We just hope when you decide to sell you will consider Clyde Realty. So call Clyde Realty at 555-8200 for your free competitive market analysis.
Clyde Realty is located at 612 West Main across from the Day-n-Night Market.

This ad mentions Clyde Realty six times. The ad should be repeated several times a day with a trial period of at least one month. It may take some time for response.

People are responsive when you appeal for help; however, the request for help should be specific. Consider the following:

Can you help a young family? Clyde Realty is looking for a three-bedroom, two-bath home with double garage, preferably on the west side for a young family transferring to our area. The father teaches grade school and the mother is an engineer. They have a seven-year-old son, a five-year-old daughter and a cocker spaniel. They are interested in a family neighborhood, preferably close to schools and would like to keep the price under $125,000. If you know of anyone having such a home for sale, please call Clyde Realty at 555-8200. That's Clyde Realty at 555-8200.

Responses to an ad like the above callers will often begin with, "Would they be interested in . . . ?" For personal appeal, use a real family, one of your salesperson's prospective buyers. Make them appear to be people your listeners would really like to know. Appeals like the above bring in listeners and are great institutional advertising tools. A word of caution: Don't overdo this appeal for help; eight or ten times a year for one week to ten days using each approach would be plenty. Also, don't over qualify buyers' needs, such as a very limited area or architectural style.

If you are knowledgeable and articulate, consider contacting a local radio station to narrate a 15- to 30-minute real estate talk show to discuss such topics as the real estate market and financing as well as to field telephone inquiries. Your office could buy several ad slots with others going to noncompetitive firms. The station gains ready-made programming, your advertising, plus allied ads from home repair, remodeling contractors, carpet cleaning, and so forth, which offer strong economic benefits to the station. With the tremendous interest in real estate, the listening audience, especially in a prime commuting time slot, should be significant. You will not only gain publicity for your firm, you will establish yourself as a local real estate expert in addition to the more direct benefits possible from your own ads during programming.

VIDEOTAPES

Some brokerage firms prepare elaborate video presentations of their properties, which are shown in their offices to prospective buyers, who are served refreshments while they view the homes. This approach has some advantages but it is our opinion that the drawbacks outweigh the benefits. One benefit is that after viewing a video if prospects are anxious to see a particular property and should that property measure up to their expectations, a sale can become a probability rather than just a possibility. The buyers "sold themselves" from viewing your video catalog.

A disadvantage is that, if prospects notice an undesirable feature or that the property does not have a feature high on their "want list," they will not want to see the property. Even an easily corrected problem such as color scheme can turn off prospective buyers. Had they visited the property, a good salesperson could have turned that negative into a positive or overcome it with other positive features. A salesperson working with a video catalog may appear to be pushy if he or she tries to influence prospects in this way before they have seen the property. Instead of helping prospects decide which homes to visit, these "sneak previews" may convince prospects not to visit any of them. Remember, while prospects are in your office, they are not in your control.

Video presentations do have their place in effective advertising. They can be used to promote properties to buyers who live a significant distance from the properties. Video presentations are often used for vacation, retirement, farm and investment properties.

Many Florida retirement developments have prospective buyers half sold before they visit by mailing out elaborate videos, which do an excellent job of selling a way of life. Generally, these videos do not sell a particular home or design.

Some Hawaiian brokers send videos of listings to Japanese brokers for their prospective buyers to view. It has been said a great number of sales are actually completed without the buyer even setting foot on the property. However, this is not the normal scenario.

Several Midwestern farm brokers send videos to cooperating brokers in Germany and Holland. After viewing videos, interested buyers visit the property with U.S. brokers usually handling sale and management aspects of the farm.

Videos can be used effectively for listings. Several firms have prepared videos to be shown to owners as to the advantages of using an agent and the advantages offered by the specific agent.

One real estate firm uses an exceptional video to obtain listings from builders. It shows the agent working with the builder making suggestions as to plan changes to help salability, and carries through with the brokers marketing efforts culminating in a successful sale. The video is a low-key yet effective approach at selling benefits.

Professionally prepared videos with skillful narrations are a worthwhile marketing tool for large developments and more expensive single properties. Firms with in-house capabilities to produce effective videos are the exception. Presentation and film techniques are important to convey the desired message in the most effective manner. Many firms do a creditable job on the video photo portion, but fail miserably on the dialogue, editing or both. How and what is said becomes as important as the wording of an ad. Consider professional help in preparing your videos. A number of advertising firms can coordinate talent for producing quality videotapes.

A secondary benefit of video sales tools, which some agents believe is more important than the sales benefit, is the listing benefit. Videos are the types of things property owners like. It shows you appreciate their property and will give it the attention the owner feels it deserves. If your competition does not use videos, videos offer you an extremely strong listing edge, regardless of their effectiveness in selling property.

MOVIE SCREENS

Movie theaters often run a group of advertisements prior to the feature film, to a captive audience. Consider the demographics of movie-goers in your area before advertising in movie theaters.

If a large percentage are young adults, singles or recently married, then products you could effectively advertise would be: rentals, smaller condominiums, and starter homes.

Unless you have a TV commercial suitable for the theater market, your production costs for movie house commercials could outweigh the benefits. Production costs could be lowered with simple use of slides and voice-overs, or a very simple video presentation. Have your presentation indicate that fliers or brochures about the property are available in the lobby. You should then have a display rack in the lobby. Commercial brochure holders are available from real estate supply firms. Having brochures available will magnify the effectiveness of your screen ads.

TELEPHONE PROMOTIONS

We all know we can use the telephone for listing solicitations, but it can be used for advertising sales as well. We can use the telephone to inform, create interest and elicit action. For example, we can call neighbors to inform them of an open house in their area. We can invite them for coffee and to see the home in the event they might have a friend who is interested in living in the neighborhood. This is pure advertising. Renters can also be solicited by telephone as possible buyers. Inviting renters to an open house or project opening is a productive telephone approach.

You can use a reverse directory, which lists occupants by street addresses first and then names and telephone numbers, for your telephone solicitations. From the address of an apartment complex you now have access to every renter, except those with unlisted telephone numbers. Consider new housing developments with a number of units and excellent low down payment financing for soliciting renters. Your telephone solicitation script for buyers on the project could be as follows:

Is this Mrs. Jenkins? I am Lillian Smith from Wright Realty. Mrs. Jenkins, have you thought about owning your own home for privacy and protection from rent increases? I am calling you because we are marketing a limited number of homes in Meadow Heights, which can be purchased with a modest down payment and payments of only $650 per month, and most of that payment will be tax deductible. Does this interest you, Mrs. Jenkins?
Meadow Heights is less than 45 minutes from the Civic Center. All homes feature three full-size bedrooms, two

baths, two-car garage, all kitchen appliances and a full fenced yard. Does this interest you, Mrs. Jenkins?
I can arrange to show these fine homes to you and your husband tomorrow at 5:30 P.M., or would 6:30 be better for you?
Are you familiar with the location of our Wright Realty office? Do you have a pencil handy? It is at 712 West Main across from the post office. Again, it is Wright Realty and I am Lillian Smith. I look forward to seeing you and your husband tomorrow at 5:30 P.M.

Worded to seek positive answers as to interest and the choice of seeing the property, this script offers only a choice as to time. The purpose is to locate possible buyers who will come to your office. You will then have the opportunity to qualify these buyers and show them other properties if needed. Your call really gives no more information than a classified ad. You want to avoid giving too much information on the telephone— just enough to bring them in.

A similar approach can be used to find income property buyers. You can obtain names and addresses of owners of similar properties in the area by checking tax rolls. Then, using the regular telephone directory, you can call an owner:

Mr. Jones, I am Lillian Smith from Wright Realty. I am calling you because you own the apartment building at 612 West Main. We have recently listed the adjacent property at 614 West Main, the 24-apartment unit to the west of your building. Are you familiar with the building? I think it presents an exceptional purchase opportunity for you because you own the adjacent building. I am certain you understand the management advantages of owning both properties. Mr. Jones, I would like to discuss this opportunity with you. I am free tomorrow afternoon. Are you available at 3 P.M. or would 4 P.M. be better for you?

Again, give very little information. What you want is a face-to-face meeting to determine needs before you go into any details about the specific property.

6   Signs and Displays

Your office sign and the For Sale sign you place on front lawns are not the only signage with which you should be concerned. Signs and displays are important elements of many advertising plans.

OUTDOOR ADVERTISING

When we use the term *outdoor advertising*, we are referring to large outdoor signs or billboards generally viewed through the windows of passing vehicles.

Billboard viewers cannot be selective, so outdoor advertising is a shotgun approach as applied to real estate advertising. On the other hand, classified ads are more targeted as they are sought out by parties who generally have some interest in the product. While radio also reaches much of the traveling market, it is far more selective than billboard advertising because of station programming.

It is possible to diminish the shotgun nature of outdoor advertising by sign placement in particular targeted areas. It is even possible to target particular ethnic groups by the selection of models for the poster. Nevertheless, the message of outdoor signs can "hit" anyone who comes within sight of it.

The Eight-Sheet Outdoor Advertising Association, Inc., cites six principles to incorporate into outdoor advertising:

1. Product identification. The advertiser's name and product must register with the viewer quickly.
2. Simple background. The background should help, not interfere with, the basic idea presented.
3. Large illustrations.
4. Legible type.
5. Bold colors.
6. Short copy. Besides short words, the idea must be expressed quickly so the reader can grasp the message at a glance.

Other outdoor advertising experts give just three rules for outdoor advertising:

1. Be Brief
2. Be Bold
3. Be Clear

In short, don't try to be subtle; your message must come across immediately.

To help you understand the effect of an outdoor display, you should plan and make a mock-up of the sign using a scale of one inch equals a foot. Now view the sign from a distance of 100 inches (about eight and one-half feet). This will give you just about the same effect as viewing the full-size billboard at 100 feet.

At highway speeds, billboards are only viewed for a few seconds, so readability is important. Use either all lowercase letters for your message or a combination of uppercase and lowercase letters. Using all capital letters or decorative type decreases readability. Especially avoid their use for long messages. Very thin or heavy type face tends to be illegible from a distance and should be avoided. Spacing between letters and words must be adequate or they will seem to run together when viewed from a distance.

For readability, the type must contrast sharply with the background color (see page 32). Color combinations to avoid are blue/green, orange/red, yellow/white and purple/blue combinations, as their lack of contrast makes messages difficult to read while traveling at high speeds.

Avoid vertical lettering. Everything should read from left to right. Many experts feel a standard billboard should not contain more than ten words. Some even place the limit at seven.

Eight-sheet outdoor ads called "junior posters," have a 5' by 11' poster area. They are generally printed (by lithography or silk-screen) on three equal sheets and pasted up much like wallpaper. Because of their small size, these posters are more effective within cities where traffic travels at slower speeds. Costs of eight-sheet billboards vary from around $60 per month to $200 per month for each billboard, depending on market and location. The average eight-sheet poster has 10,000 selling impressions per day or 300,000 per month, and is sold for 30-day periods. Eight-sheet billboards are probably the lowest-cost mass marketing advertising approach in terms of cost per viewer.

The standard outdoor billboard is the 24-sheet poster. The billboard is 12' by 25', with a net area of 104 by 234 inches.

Location and market will affect the cost of billboards. A lighted sign would cost more. Painted billboards cost considerably more than billboards pasted up with lithographed sheets

FIGURE 6.1 Billboard Silhouette

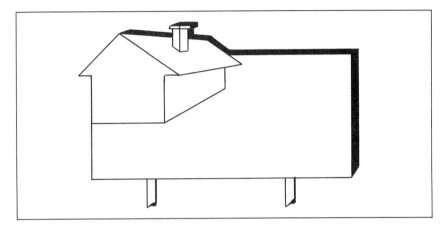

and are generally lighted. Because painted billboards are more expensive, they are not changed as often as paper posted boards.

You can get photographs for billboards. While the effect can be spectacular, the photo costs for a billboard can run in the $10,000 range. The high cost makes it impractical for most real estate promotional use.

Embellishments or silhouettes are possible at additional cost. This makes the billboard stand out from other rectangular signs. As an example, the peak of a house could protrude over the top of the billboard as in figure 6.1.

Special effects such as animated billboards, special glitter paint, and so on, are all available for an additional cost. Motion billboards with changing messages could cost significantly more per month.

Bulletins are the large billboards you see on major highways. They are 14' by 48' and can be effective even at highway speeds. Bulletins are generally painted. They create a dramatic presence by their sheer size. Bulletin costs vary by location and customarily would range from around $1,000 to $5,000 per month with special effects priced extra.

In many advertising marketing areas, a relatively small percentage of the highways carry the bulk of daily traffic. For instance, 20 percent of the highways might typically carry 85 percent of daily traffic. These are the desirable locations for billboards and the cost would reflect the traffic. Billboards at locations where the traffic flow is slow are the most effective because of the longer period of message impact on viewers.

When reviewing locations offered when buying billboard space, consider the background of the billboard. Does it stand out or is it cluttered? Also consider driver distractions. A billboard right after a danger or curve sign will probably result in the driver's eyes being peeled to the road.

You will have to pay for printing or painting in addition to your monthly fee. Contracts are generally for at least three months. You can rotate your ads by changing billboard locations every three months. This will appear to increase your presence in the marketplace. With a rotary plan, your painted billboard face is actually removed and placed in a different location. This avoids the duplication of painting costs.

In using billboards we speak of GRP (gross rating points), the effective daily circulation generated divided by market population. Therefore, signs viewed by 500,000 people daily in a 1,000,000 person market would give you a #50 showing.

Because of the cost and time involved in preparing billboards, they are not an effective tool to market a single home. However, they are an excellent tool for marketing a subdivision as well as your firm.

A series of billboards can even be used to create interest and to finally direct the traffic off the highway to a development. They can be used in conjunction with ads or even to attract visitors looking for other developments. Billboards can announce grand openings and even sell price and terms to bring in traffic.

Billboard companies offer a large selection of stock posters much like the clip art available from newspapers. These posters can be customized with your name or project name. We suggest you avoid stock posters, as the result may be less than you could obtain with a billboard designed for your particular needs.

Figure 6.2 offers examples of billboards used to sell particular projects:

FIGURE 6.2   Billboard Ads

FIGURE 6.2   Billboard Ads (continued)

Source: Naegele Outdoor Advertising, Inc. Reprinted with permission.

The outside of bus shelters provide space for mini-billboards for passing motorists as well as pedestrians and those waiting for public transportation. However, an estimated 90 percent of shelter viewers are part of the vehicular traffic. Generally, bus shelters are in prime traffic locations. Bus shelter ads are available in at least 25 major markets as well as a number of smaller market areas.

Bus shelters are usually free of competing messages so viewers have a long time to absorb the messages. Bus shelter advertising has been successfully used to promote rentals at large projects, sales of new developments and to promote the image of brokers. The bus shelter ads in figure 6.3 were used in the Minneapolis/St. Paul, Minnesota, market.

Bus benches are also an excellent advertising medium. Usually long-term and seldom changed, the messages normally reflect institutional advertising rather than promote a particular development.

The positive effect of outdoor advertising is illustrated by a drugstore in the small town of Wall, South Dakota. By use of outdoor signs, the store grew to a megastore that has catered to millions of tourists.

TRAVELING ADS

How would you like a high-visibility billboard that travels with you? The Seville Corporation of Overland Park, Kansas, has just such a billboard. It is a large recreation vehicle painted bright orange. The vehicle stands out from other vehicles on the road, and the color ties in with The Seville Corporation's For Sale signs, cards and stationery. The vehicle, bearing company name and logo, is identified as the firm's "Real Estate Sales Information Center" (figure 6.4). Such a vehicle adds tremendous visibility to tract and open house sales.

The Seville Corporation also uses this vehicle to pick up prospective buyers at hotels and airports for showing property. A relaxing atmosphere for the prospective buyers, it serves as a mobile closing room. Imagine the impact on property owners, neighbors and even other agents when your office crew uses such a mobile billboard for caravaning. The mobile unit provides strong institutional advertising, adds visibility to particular property, and even serves as an excellent salesperson recruitment tool. As a variance on The Seville Corporation's Real Estate Sales Information Center, you could use it as an "open house mobile." This unit would be a helpful and interest-

FIGURE 6.3   Bus Shelter Ads

Bus shelter ads, because of their exposure, give a broker strong name identification.

Source: Transtop. Reprinted with permission.

FIGURE 6.4   Seville Corporation's Real Estate Sales Information Center

Source: Seville Corporation, REALTOR®. Reprinted with permission.

ing approach in areas limiting signs and flags for an open house.

Travel trailers can be used as stationary billboards, and double as sales offices for subdivision sales before the homes are completed (figure 6.5). Some firms paint the project name and "advance sales office" or "pre-completion sales office" on the trailers. Then they use billboards, balloons and flags to attract additional attention to the sales office. In a good market, it is not unusual for a subdivision to sell out with advance reservations before the models are ready for showing.

Cartop carrier signs are also a very effective method of directing buyers to an open house, especially where signs cannot otherwise be placed (figure 6.6). Several commercial cartop

FIGURE 6.5   Travel Trailer Ads

FIGURE 6.6   Cartop Carrier with Sign

signs are available with space for inserting masonite signs, but many cartop carriers can be readily adapted to hold signs.

Some subdivision sales offices place a large sign on a boat trailer and tow it to the desired spot (figure 6.7). These signs are larger than car signs. A 6′ by 12′ sign is not unusual. One problem with these types of signs is that they are often ruined by being blown over in high-wind areas.

Truck Ads

You have probably seen many large city delivery trucks with no advertising on them. To the wholesalers, jobbers, manufacturers, or truck lessees, advertising might not serve any real benefit. However, in a number of large cities, billboard companies are utilizing this nonproductive space. Lease arrangements are made with the truck owners for advertising on the sides of the trucks, which is then sold to advertisers. Just a few local delivery trucks can actually provide you with traveling signs to significantly increase your firm's visibility. Such ads can either

FIGURE 6.7   Ad on Two-Wheel Trailer

Grand Opening
Pinewood Estates
Turn Left 1000 Feet

advertise a particular development or serve as institutional advertisements.

Taxi Ads

Rear signs on taxis are primarily viewed by drivers behind them. Signs on the roof of taxis are only seen by passersby. Because of space limitations, taxi ads seldom effectively sell benefits of a particular property. Such ads serve more as institutional advertising and are not very cost-effective for real estate firms. Similar benefits can be achieved at a fraction of the cost with a sign on your own autos.

Transit Ads

Your eyes scan the myriad transit ads while standing holding a strap on a bus or trolley. You find yourself reading the ads because there is nothing else to do.

Generally, transit ad cards are 11″ by 28″, although 42″ and 56″ lengths are available. End posters may be larger in size. Copy on these ads should be large enough to be read from a distance of 15 feet. Seated passengers read cards at an upward angle. Because of this, some advertisers set an attention-getting heading at the bottom of their transit ads.

You can target specific areas by purchasing transit card space on particular routes. A full run is one card in every bus or trolley, a double run is two cards in every bus or trolley while one-half of a run is one card in half of the cars.

Transit ad cards are very low priced per viewer. They can contain a great deal more copy than billboards, since passengers view transit cards for a longer period of time. Advertising can also be placed on the exterior of buses and trolleys with front, rear and side posters. However, for ads on the outside of a moving bus, copy should not run longer than the seven to ten words recommended for a billboard, due to a relatively short viewing time.

Transit advertising is more of a supplemental advertising medium than a primary market medium. Approximately 80 percent of long-time users of transit ads are local businesses, and the majority are long-time users of the advertising medium.

"Take one" tear sheet pads can be attached to interior transit ad cards. A postcard tear sheet can be effective in bringing in responses; however, in some areas they have been removed by vandals and dropped in postal boxes, resulting in the advertiser paying the postal charges to receive blank cards.

Because of printing costs, the time from inception to display, and a minimum 30-day insertion, transit ads are not appropriate for advertising a particular home, but large developments, rentals or institutional advertising are suited to this ad medium.

In some areas, your best results with this type of advertising is probably with housing developments offering low down payments and lower total costs. This is not true in all areas. In central business districts, many middle- to high-income workers and shoppers often use public transportation. In such cases, higher-priced developments can be effectively advertised.

The message on your transit card is more important than the artwork, since the message will be read regardless of its design. Your message must be strong enough for the reader to make a mental note of what is advertised or, better yet, take a tear-off sheet or card stating the project's location or how to obtain further information.

BULLETIN BOARDS

You will find public bulletin boards in supermarkets, Laundromats, senior centers, public buildings, and so on. Many people can't pass by a bulletin board without checking its contents. One advantage of advertising on bulletin boards is they are *free*. It is hard to realize that many people, especially some younger adults, do not regularly read newspapers. Bulletin boards are just one of the ways you can reach this segment of the market.

Laundromat bulletin boards are particularly effective ways to advertise. A property brief or just a 3″ × 5″ or 5″ × 7″ card can be attached to a bulletin board. The most effective housing units to advertise in Laundromat areas would be smaller homes or condominiums for rent or sale. The majority of people frequenting most laundromats are from a one- to two-person household, although not necessarily in the low-income bracket.

Other bulletin boards can be used effectively to cover a wide range of housing and even investment property. Some boards, controlled by stores, require that notices be a certain size; in some cases approval must be obtained before posting notices. Most, however, have few if any restrictions. You should, however, always indicate on your notices that you are an agent. Figure 6.8 shows examples of these notices.

As you can see, the 5″ × 7″ card is much more effective, as it is larger than the 3″ × 5″ card. The 5″ × 7″ size has room for a photograph, and the copy stands out.

In addition to attracting buyers, bulletin boards can be an excellent source of listing leads. You will find that owners advertise their own properties on these bulletin boards. Often, these owners have not yet placed newspaper ads.

FIGURE 6.8 Bulletin Board Notices

5″ × 7″ format

3 BR Home — Hillside School

Huge double garage, child-safe fenced yard, full basement,
fruit trees and a neighborhood you will love.

Only $89,500
$3,000 Down

Call

Henry Jones at
Clyde Realty
555-8200
Eve: 555-3173

Color Photograph
of Property

3″ × 5″ format

3 BR Home — Hillside School

Huge double garage, child-safe fenced yard, full basement,
fruit trees and a neighborhood you will love.

Only $89,500
$3,000 Down

Your Business Card

AIRPORT AND BUS STATION DISPLAYS

Display cases at airports and bus stations get excellent exposure. Costs of display space at major airports would likely make advertising impractical for all but multi-office firms. However, smaller airports offer relatively inexpensive advertising display space.

Advertisements should display office as well as evening telephone numbers prominently. Displays should be updated regularly, including color photographs, information and prices on properties. You should use a rack attachment for business cards and handout material on properties for rent or for sale. If there is a small airport in your community without display cases, you might consider contacting airport management about your installing display units (either as a free standing unit or against a wall). A reasonable rent should be possible if you are installing the display cases. If you can't get permission to use display cases, most airports have information areas or booths where Chamber of Commerce types of material are available. You should be able to obtain permission to place your office printed material—newsletters, property briefs or pamphlets—in these information areas or booths, or even install your own commercial racks to hold your handout material.

Bus depots are a better source of rentals than sales. Rental information, especially of furnished rentals, can be effectively promoted in this manner. Your material should emphasize how to get to the rental (include public transportation information, if available), as well as the necessary telephone numbers.

INFORMATION BOOTHS

Did you ever think of selling real estate at a swap meet? Well, one large Palm Desert, California, brokerage firm does, and does it effectively. They have set up a real estate information booth with displays showing color photographs of their properties (figure 6.9).

In talking with their salespeople, we learned that servicing the booth was considered sought-after uptime. Many prospective buyers and sellers hesitate to walk into a brokerage office, yet these booths present a nonthreatening opportunity to discuss ideas on selling, buying or leasing property with real estate professionals. By offering a free competitive market analysis, an easy entree is possible for a listing. Expecting only interest in less expensive properties, the salespeople were surprised to discover a cross-section of contacts ranging from minimal housing to million-dollar homes and investment properties. While the booth attracts many people who merely want to talk to pass the time of day, the firm's salespeople have found plenty of real leads including walk-ins asking agents to list their property. A booth such as this should be staffed by several agents, as there is plenty of action.

Some firms set up booths or kiosks at local fairs and in malls. If your community plans a street sale and your office is on a major shopping street, moving a booth complete with displays outside your office can be highly productive. It invites discussions with interested parties in a nonthreatening environment.

FIGURE 6.9   Real Estate Promotion Booth at Swap Meet

Source: Hampton REALTORS®. Reprinted with permission.

7   Direct-Mail Advertising

We all know people who say they throw out all junk mail. Some even say they don't even open junk mail. Nevertheless, over 90 percent of direct-mail pieces are opened and hardly a family in this nation has not responded positively at some time to mail solicitations. Junk mail is unwanted solicitations. After reading your mailings, it is hoped buyers and sellers do not find them to be unwanted.

Reaching prospective buyers and sellers through their mailboxes has the highest cost per thousand contacts of any advertising approach. The high cost of direct mail is offset by the fact that direct mail offers the highest response rate per thousand contacts. What is really important is not the advertising price per contact but the advertising price per response.

THE ENVELOPE

Responses can be increased by following a few simple rules:

- *Stamps.* Don't use a postage machine or a bulk mailing permit. If your mailing piece looks like junk mail, it will likely be treated as junk mail. The greatest response is from letters using first-class stamps, and commemorative stamps will give you greater response than regular stamps. Studies have shown that people are likely to open letters with commemorative stamps first and spend more time with the mailing piece.
- *Envelope.* Don't use a window envelope, as it makes your mailer look like junk mail.

You are a professional. Don't engage in unethical practices of making your mailing appear to be what it isn't. Don't use an envelope that appears to be a government notification. Don't use an envelope that makes your mailing appear to be a certified or special-delivery letter, or even a telegram. Don't use a window envelope and make your solicitation appear to be a check. Even a hint of deception must be avoided. You are selling a very personal and professional service. Deception will backfire on you by creating bad will rather than goodwill.

A plain, number-ten envelope without a return address or a handwritten return address must be opened. A letter with a broker's name on it might be trashed unopened. Curiosity requires that an unmarked letter be opened. Many brokers use this technique.

Some direct-mail advertisers use an undersized envelope to make their letter appear to be a personal one. The problem is that your flier must either be reduced in size or else it will require awkward folding. In addition, this technique has been overworked in many areas, reducing its effectiveness.

Don't use preprinted mailing labels. They practically shout "junk mail!" Handwrite (which is preferable) or type addresses. Never send a letter to an "Occupant." You are just asking for it to be trashed. If you want to cover an area, use a reverse directory or property tax list so your letters can be sent to individuals.

THE MESSAGE

An invitation is an excellent direct-mail approach. The invitation should be on a heavier stock, preferably with formal raised print. It should appear similar to a wedding invitation. You can use the invitation approach for an open house, grand opening, pre-grand opening or even the opening of a new office. A pre-grand opening has a certain snob appeal, as it appears to be for a selective group.

By adding "RSVP" to openings such as a "champagne pre-grand opening," you make the invitation appear more personal. People will regard the invitation as more exclusive and the result should be a higher response than if RSVP had been omitted.

For a direct-mail piece to be effective, it must gain the reader's attention. You have only a few seconds to do this. If the heading gains the reader's attention and the first 25 words hold the attention, then your message will be read. Don't worry about having too much copy, as you now have the reader. Some of the most effective mailing pieces ever produced have had over 1,000 words. Your reader will continue unless there is something in the copy that turns him or her off.

You want your mailing piece to appear to be as personal as possible. If you type a name into a preprinted letter, it had better match perfectly. It cannot appear to be a form letter, or the chances of it being trashed will be significantly increased.

The best direct-mailing piece heading promises a benefit. One benefit is that something is free. Headings can intrigue the reader, such as a statement that is utterly outrageous, a statement the reader must agree with or even humor. However, the copy must come to the point rather quickly while supporting that point.

Keep in mind, however, that homeowners are bombarded with mailing pieces from other real estate offices vying for listings. To be effective, your mailing piece must stand out from the competition, get attention and give a message the reader welcomes. As an example, all homeowners are interested in the value of their home especially when the market is rising. Homeowners like to know what their major asset is worth. Information on area sales will be read. Information selling benefits will be read.

Testimonials impress people. Consider an attachment of several pages of testimonial letters. The simplest way to get letters is to ask buyers and sellers at the conclusion of a sale for a letter of recommendation you can use in your advertising.

Some brokers have and use many such letters from owners who sold in specific areas as testimonials to obtain listings in those same areas. This is a strong persuader, especially when the reader knows the seller, the property or both. The fact that other people do it has weight. Besides using this in your testimonials, you could point out that most For Sale by Owner signs are replaced with agents' signs because owners trying to sell their property by themselves seldom succeed.

When adding attachments to a basic letter, you might have to consider using a lighter weight envelope and paper, since exceeding one ounce could be costly in terms of postage.

Lists work well with direct mail. Numbered lists tend to be read:

Ten reasons why Cliff Heights is the finest residential area in Madison County:

1. Estate-sized lots
2. Streets, sidewalks, curb and gutter installed and paid for
3. Complete landscaping included
4. Quality homes with wood-burning fireplaces, 2- to 3-car garages, 2 to 2½ baths and all Maytag appliances
5. Walking distance to Midvale School
6. Nine minutes to Midvale Mall
7. Six golf courses within 15 minutes
8. Only four minutes to the freeway
9. Low-down financing that's hard to believe
10. Prices starting at just $139,500

In writing copy, you might wish to include real-life stories. People like stories. You could use stories of success (where an owner used you as an agent) and horror stories of failure or problems when they tried to sell their own property. Don't invent stories; there are too many good ones around. Write in an informal manner, as if you were talking to a friend. Short sentences and commonly used words should be the rule. Avoid script or novelty type faces, as it makes your mailing piece difficult to read.

After you have written your copy, we recommend that you let it marinate—in other words, let it sit for a few days. Look at it later in different surroundings at a different time of day. For some reason or another you will quickly see logical improvements or even whole new approaches that would make your mailer more effective. Some copywriters believe that we subconsciously think about what we have done, explaining why some difficult problems are solved easily after we set them aside.

ELICITING ACTION

You want action from your mailing in the form of a call or letter. You want to make these actions as easy as possible. If you desire a letter, include a self-addressed envelope with a mailing indicia (a box in place of a stamp, indicating that you will pay postage). To use a mailing indicia, see your postmaster for a permit application and printing requirements. If you want telephone calls from outside your area, include a toll-free "800" number. This is far more effective than asking callers to call you collect (see Section on "800" numbers in Chapter 3).

A far more effective approach than asking the recipient to call or write is a statement that you will be calling them in a few days. This forces readers to consider what you have said and what their response will be. The recipient cannot just disregard your letter when this approach is used, as they know you will be calling.

One of the most effective direct-mail pieces we have ever seen was used by a real estate salesperson who specializes in listings. She sends it to owners who are trying to sell their own homes. She attaches a new one-dollar bill to a letter which says:

I Can Save You Money

I am going to show you how to save thousands of these one dollar bills. I will be calling you in the next few days to set up a brief appointment. I hope you can spare just a few minutes to save thousands of dollars.

This particular salesperson says that she gets an appointment 40 to 50 percent of the time. She figures her listing percentage at about one out of four appointments, or one out of about ten letters.

While it takes guts to mail out money, the technique works for her. It must be said that she is a superb, professional salesperson and comes to her presentations fully prepared to succeed. Her mailing earns her a positive reaction from callers, and her telephone skill gets her in the door. The benefits she offers give her listing success. Incidentally, she pointed out that, with the price of stamps today, a one dollar bill is by far the least expensive way to go, and what better way is there to get a person's attention than by giving them money.

Another agent attached a quarter to each letter asking recipients to call the broker. The results were dismal. Apparently, most recipients simply removed the quarter and threw the letter away. The approach was poor because it required the recipient to contact the agent rather than telling the recipient the agent would be contacting them.

Most responses to mail solicitations will be within ten days of receipt, but there will be a small residual response, which may come months later. Direct-mail marketers often receive responses years after the offer was originally made. Also keep in mind that direct mail has an institutional advertising effect.

Always test-market a new mailing before any mass mailing. By test-marketing controlled numbers, it is possible to evaluate how copy changes affect response effect. By keying different copy to different salespeople, you can evaluate percentages of response.

Advertising is somewhat scientific but it is also very much an art. What we are certain will be effective often is not. One nationally known advertising executive evaluated a mailing piece we developed for a client that was getting a 9 percent response. The response rate for similar mailings was less than 3 percent. The executive, who did not know about our success, told our client why the mailing piece would be unsuccessful. In fact, he said it was just "poor advertising." While the executive knew advertising in theory, our mailing piece had been developed in practice, after using more than 50 different mailing pieces over a period of nine months to achieve our results.

HIDDEN OPPORTUNITIES

If your office handles property management, chances are you mail out rent receipts to tenants each month. Since you have the mailing costs anyway, you should consider what else could be included. As an example, you could include material on and applications for tenant insurance coverage. You can go up to one ounce without any additional postal cost, so take advantage of it. When ordering printing keep in mind that after the first 1,000 copies, the price per thousand should drop significantly as the set-up costs have been taken care of. The additional cost should be material and press time. If you are quoted the same price per thousand for additional pieces, you should consider obtaining competitive bids. Have your printer fold your pieces for you. A folding machine does the job neatly and at far less than the cost of the cheapest hand labor.

Unfortunately, some real estate sales firms have crossed the ethical line. You have probably seen mailings from land sales and time share firms stating you have won one of the Category A prizes. In Category A, the three prizes are a Rolls-Royce convertible, a 38-foot yacht and a Jobormota sound system. Category B prizes are all cars and Category C are simple prizes such as a 42-inch television. The mailing probably required that you attend a 90-minute presentation to collect your gift. If you attended the presentation, you would likely receive a sound system that clips on your belt with a wire to your ear. This type of advertising negatively reflects on the entire real estate profession and makes it more difficult for legitimate brokers to use the mail effectively. Nevertheless, the mail is an effective advertising medium if used properly.

Figure 7.1 shows sample direct-mailing pieces from *Power Real Estate Letters* (Real Estate Education Company).

FIGURE 7.1   Sample Direct-Mail Pieces

Homer Fink Saves Thousands

Homer Fink is selling his home without an agent so he can save the agent's fee for himself. Homer is a pretty smart guy.

Of course, Homer stays home every evening and weekends waiting for the phone to ring, or the doorbell to buzz. Homer doesn't mind, as it keeps him from being out spending money and it gives his life a purpose, that of selling his home.

Homer can't understand why most of his hot prospects fail to return and talk of deals never ends up on paper. Nevertheless, Homer has faith that Mr. and Mrs. Right will come along. Anyway, he can always sell to the gentleman in the blue suede shoes who offered to trade him stock in an emerald mine.

If you want to be like Homer we wish you luck, but if you really want to sell, give some consideration to what I have to say when I call you in a few days.

[*Henry Wilson*]
[*Associate Broker*]
[*Clyde Realty*]   [*555-8200*]

FIGURE 7.1   Sample Direct-Mail Pieces (continued)

[Date]

_____

_____

_____

Dear _____ :

When we listed the [24-unit apartment building at 3305–3307 Chestnut Boulevard], I immediately thought this would be the ideal investment for the owner of the property at [3309 Chestnut Boulevard].

Because the property [is right next door to your property] [is so close to your property and is so similar], the management advantages of dual ownership are readily apparent.

The property is available at [an attractive price with flexible terms][$1.5 million with approximately $150,000 down] [a price and terms that will allow an immediate positive cash flow]. I will be calling you in the next few days to discuss the advantages this fine property can offer you.

Yours truly,

_____

P.S.: If you are not interested in purchasing this property, perhaps you would consider selling your property. The advantages to a buyer owning both properties could make for an exceptional sale opportunity.

NOTE: _The P.S. raises the interesting switch that if the reader isn't a buyer, then he or she should be a seller. It also reinforces the advantages of owning the two properties._

FIGURE 7.1   Sample Direct-Mail Pieces (continued)

> # SOLD
>
> Is this the sign in front of your home? Or is it simply,
>
> For Sale
> By Owner
>
> The likelihood of turning the second sign into the first sign is very slim, which explains why most For Sale By Owner signs are replaced by broker's signs.
>
> Did you realize that:
>
> 1. most calls on For Sale By Owner signs are from people who can't afford the home they are calling on?
>
> 2. most calls from newspaper ads are from people who would not be satisfied with a home priced in the range they inquired about?
>
> Without an inventory to move inquiries up or down, most of an owner's effort ends up wasted.
>
> I will call you in the next few days, not to try to saddle you with agent selling fees, but to show you how I can help you have more money in your pocket after a sale.
>
> Isn't what you actually net more important than anything else?
>
> [*Tom Haskins*]
> [*Sales Associate*]
> [*Clyde Realty*]   [*555-8200*]

FIGURE 7.1   Sample Direct-Mail Pieces (continued)

No Agent = No Commission

That seems like a good reason to try to sell without an agent—except that "no agent" usually means "no sale." That explains why most For Sale By Owner signs are replaced by agent signs.

I will be calling you in the next few days to show you not only the dangers of owner sales, but the positive benefits we can offer. If I can show you how I can put more money in your pockets, will you want to talk with me?

[*Joe Schmidt*]
[*Clyde Realty*]   [*555-8200*]

NOTE: *This is a short and effective letter. It grabs the reader's attention and states a common owner belief. Asking if the reader will talk to you to find out how to make more money from the sale of a home makes it hard to say no. When you call, you might say, "[Mr. Smith], I wrote you the other day and told you I would call. My letter asked if I could show you how I could put more money in your pockets—would you want to talk with me? I would like to show [both you and Mrs. Smith] how I will accomplish this. Will [both you and Mrs. Smith] be home [tonight at 7:00 P.M.], or would [8:00 P.M.] be more convenient?"*

The choice given above is to time, not if they will talk with you. When you meet them, you would use material from Power Real Estate Listing *[Dearborn], to show the seller the financial benefits of listing with your office.*

FIGURE 7.1 Sample Direct-Mail Pieces (continued)

**Why Are Most For Sale By Owner Signs Replaced
by Agent Signs?
Because Agents Sell!**

Utilizing an agent means:

- You are protected against unscrupulous buyers hoping to pay less than market value for your home.

- No unescorted, unqualified persons will enter your home.

- Contracts are likely to end in a sale—not in a courtroom.

- You are able to meet buyer financing needs.

- You are no longer a prisoner in your own home waiting for the bell to ring.

- You are more likely to sell your home.

- The sale will result in a higher net to you.

Think about it. I will be calling you in the next few days to answer any questions you might have and to prove everything I have said.

[*Tom Jones*]
[*Clyde Realty*]   [*555-8200*]

FIGURE 7.1   Sample Direct-Mail Pieces (continued)

Can You Help a Neighbor?

We need a 3-bedroom home in your neighborhood for a [*young family*]. The [*husband is an engineer and the wife is a school teacher. They have a son 11 years old and a daughter who is seven. They would like to relocate prior to school in September and desire a home within walking distance of Midvale School*].

If you know of any friends or neighbors who might consider selling their home to this young family, we would appreciate hearing from you.

Sincerely,

[*Bob Jones*]
[*Clyde Realty*]

NOTE: *The heading should get this missive read. The family should be a real family with whom you are working, and they should be pictured in a very positive manner. People will go out of their way to help specific people, but not people in general. This is not only an effective listing canvassing tool, but the effort expended for the family you are working for will serve to make them feel indebted to you, reducing the chances of them contacting another agent.*

FIGURE 7.1 Sample Direct-Mail Pieces (continued)

Pretty Young Girl

who wants desperately to get married and start a family, has finally found a suitable mate.

Her problem is she has no place to keep him. If you would be willing to sell a [*3BR Westside home with a garage for $160,000 or less*], please call me immediately. The alternative is spinsterhood.

[*Tom Flynn, Sales Associate*]
[*Clyde Realty*]
[*555-8200*]

NOTE: *A light solicitation flier such as this for a particular buyer can be extremely effective. It is likely to be read and talked about.*

And, as with the previous letter, make sure you get permission from the "pretty young girl" before you use this tactic.

A better approach for these last two letters would be to indicate you will be the one calling.

Source: *Power Real Estate Letters.* Copyright 1990, Dearborn Financial Publishing, Inc. Published by Real Estate Education Company, a division of Dearborn Financial Publishing, Inc., Chicago.

8 Additional Media Considerations

While it may seem as though we have covered all the advertising media available for residential real estate promotion, additional media can play a significant role in your overall advertising plan.

MAGAZINES

Generally, magazines are not suitable for residential real estate advertising, as the circulation area is usually greater than the real estate firm's market area. This could result in costs exceeding benefits. Exceptions are society magazines centered in a particular city; these generally include local fashion ads and all-color photographs. Such magazines can be an excellent advertising medium for luxury homes and developments because of the high income of the average reader.

Special-interest magazines can be used for marketing property appealing to special interests. For instance, a home with a large kennels advertised in a dog magazine, or land zoned for a salvage yard advertised in an appropriate trade magazine. Specialty properties are more likely to draw buyers from a larger geographical area than would regular residential properties.

HOME MAGAZINES

Free magazines devoted to property being offered for sale are proliferating across the country. These area magazines are either published by a single broker (often a multi-office firm or franchise), a local REALTOR® association or by an independent publisher who sells space and distributes the magazine. Some home magazines are specialized such as magazines devoted to new housing developments only. The size is usually 8½″ × 11″, although some are smaller. While some of these magazines are black and white with color only on the cover, a growing proportion of them are using color throughout the contents.

Property magazines are often bimonthly or quarterly although many are now monthly. They are offered free in racks at supermarkets, motels, drugstores, chamber of commerce offices and even free in newspaper vending machines.

Ads in these magazines are worthwhile and are especially productive in resort and retirement types of communities where buyers may not have established a relationship with a particular agent. These ads produce buyers for the length of the distribution and longer, as they are more likely than other print advertising to be kept for perusal.

Generally, a broker purchases a full page or more and uses it to advertise a number of properties with photos. Great care should be taken to make certain your photos reproduce well. You should consider professional photographic work. You want the best possible in such a magazine, as your photos have competition. The house details should be written like a classified ad. You want to get the reader's attention, interest, desire and action.

Properties sell quickly in a seller's market, often before the publication date. This is fine. What you really want is action: to get the reader to call or visit your office. You will then have the opportunity to switch to a property that "has just become available."

FREE WEEKLY PAPERS

Free weekly papers reach not only people who don't subscribe to newspapers, but also those looking for bargains (which includes most of us) as well as for particular items.

An advantage these papers have over major newspapers is that you can more readily match your advertising coverage to your market area. Most free weekly papers have different editions for different areas, allowing you to set your sight for your market—otherwise known as a *rifle approach*. The effectiveness of free weekly papers can be seen by the fact that in many areas, the number of classified ads has decreased in daily papers, yet increased in free weekly papers.

Generally, free weekly papers mix the ads. Therefore, readers with a specific need are forced to scan page after page of ads for a wide variety of products and services. While many of the real estate ads in these papers are For Sale By Owners, you can effectively use this relatively low-cost local marketing tool. Your heading is very important as, you want to hook a reader out of a whole sea of ads (See Chapter 4).

You should also consider placing display ads in free weekly papers. For a relatively low cost, display ads can give you the appearance of having a major market presence and have proven very effective in bringing in responses for agents placing these ads.

A few developers have discovered these papers and have found them cost-effective. One developer used a coupon for a free gift to test the medium and was amazed with the positive results achieved.

NEWSPAPER INSERTS

You can generally have fliers and other inserts delivered with the daily paper for less than the cost of a mailing.

Newspapers (including free weekly papers) will insert your piece in their papers for a charge per thousand. The inserts can sell a new subdivision or groups of particular homes, and can often be bought for a particular geographical area to match your market.

FOREIGN LANGUAGE NEWSPAPERS

Large metropolitan areas often have a number of foreign language newspapers catering to particular ethnic groups. Advertising costs per reader are generally higher than for large daily papers because of the relatively small readership. Nevertheless, foreign language papers are often well suited for real estate advertising.

Because of language barriers, these papers often have less cross-readership than do competing English language papers. If you have one or more salespersons conversant in the foreign language, you should consider placing your ad in the language of the group as well as indicating who speaks the language at your firm. If you don't speak the language, your ad should be in English.

Consider using a foreign language paper to advertise a property in an area that group might consider desirable. In this manner, your ad takes on a directed rifle approach, using a medium likely to be read by the ultimate purchaser. You must also include properties in other areas in your ad; otherwise, you could be guilty of *"steering,"* or directing ethnic groups to specific areas, which is unethical and illegal.

FOREIGN NEWSPAPERS

If you have large prestigious properties that are likely to appeal to foreign investors, you should consider foreign advertising. Japanese buyers, in particular, have played a key role in many market areas. In Hawaii, Japanese buyers have purchased homes, condominiums and investment properties. Japanese purchases on the U.S. mainland have been primarily large resort and investment properties.

It is possible to reach these buyers by advertising in Japanese newspapers in Japan. A U.S. advertising agency, Hori & Bunker, Inc. (1-800-USA-2111) acts as an agent for *Nihon Keizai Shimbun,* Japan's largest business daily newspaper. They handle advertising for the international edition of NKS. Hori & Bunker also produce *International Real Estate News.* They publish a monthly edition in Japanese and a quarterly edition in English, which is distributed worldwide.

If you do any foreign advertising you will have a powerful tool for listing large properties. Because your competitors likely have never advertised abroad, having foreign ads in your listing presentation material will set you apart from other brokerage firms. Most Americans believe foreign buyers to be synonymous with high prices. Regardless of whether this is true, your experience in foreign marketing will put you one up on your competition.

TELEPHONE DIRECTORIES

At the very least, you want people who know your firm name to be able to contact your firm by telephone. This necessitates a local telephone directory listing. You should be listed in both the yellow and white pages of the directory. Consider the following categories available in the yellow pages:

- Apartment finding and rental services
- Appraisers
- Property Management
- Real Estate
- Real Estate Appraisals
- Real Estate Consultants
- Real Estate Investments
- Real Estate Management
- Real Estate Rental Service

Today, there is more than one commercial telephone directory. While the bulk of your advertising costs should be in the dominant telephone directory, you should at least be listed in other available directories. Competitive directories may have exceptional rates, which compensate for lower usage. If so, you should consider the same coverage as the dominant directory.

If regular typed listings are being used by your competition, consider boldfaced, dark listings (for both yellow and white pages—if available). If the competition is using boldfaced type, use a small block ad within the alphabetical column to make your listing appear more impressive. A block ad in the alphabetical columns can be more effective than a large display ad on another page.

Many telephone directories allow for the use of color in an ad (primarily red). You could box your ad and highlight it with red ink. This of course costs extra. If a great many of your competitors already use highlighting, then using color will be less effective. Unless the additional cost is nominal, you may as well just use black for your listings.

You might want to consider a display ad depending on the percentage of business you receive from your yellow pages listing. Display ads are much more important for specific services than for general real estate. For example, a person might hire an appraisal firm from a telephone directory but would be far less likely to choose a broker to help buy or sell from a display ad in the yellow pages.

If you wish to insert a display ad in the yellow pages, make sure you or the design firm you use fully understands the directory firm's policies. Because some directory firms have border limitations and restrictions on reverse ads, screens and prices, your ad may appear different than you imagine.

Unfortunately, people who sell directory ads are often seasonal workers paid by commissions. At times they are not fully informed as to yellow page policy or make any statements and promises they consider necessary to make a sale. Get directory guidelines and restrictions in writing.

Personnel from yellow page firms will want to handle production of your display ad—don't let them. They use clip art, which means your ads can end up looking the same as your competitor's. Spend the few extra dollars to use your logo and the style used in your other display advertising of your directory ads. Again, don't use photos. They reproduce horribly in the yellow pages. Line drawings will appear far more impressive and work very well.

Be aware of the deadlines for yellow page advertising, as they are strictly applied. Any changes in your ads must be made in a timely fashion. Ask for proofs, because after the directory is printed it is too late to complain about the use of an old telephone number in your ads.

For offices in major metropolitan areas, consider foreign language telephone directories. Since most real estate professionals don't know such directories exist, your listing could be very valuable, especially if you have a salesperson who speaks the particular language.

PRESS RELEASES

Press releases provide valuable free publicity about your firm, staff, accomplishments and properties listed or sold.

Some large offices hire public relations firms to handle their press releases, but in most offices the person who writes ads also prepares press releases. Unfortunately, opportunities are often lost using in-house personnel who either do not realize the newsworthiness of an item or allow other work to interfere with writing quality press releases. While relatively simple to write, press releases that provide answers for *who? what? why?* and *where?* plus the additional *How?* are all too often given low priority in favor of something more urgent.

Photographs accompanying press releases should tell a story. As an example, a press release with a photo of a major sale or lease could be a buyer and seller (or lessor and lessee) shaking hands with the broker looking on, along with the broker's sign complete with a Sold or Leased strip prominently displayed.

Press release photos should be either 5″ × 7″ or 8″ × 10″ inch black-and-white glossies. Attach the caption with rubber cement or masking tape so that it flaps down from the back of the photograph and can be easily read by the editor. The accompanying press release should be written so that a newspaper can use it unedited.

The more advertising you place with a newspaper, the better your chances are every press release will be printed. This is a basic fact of life. The real estate sections of a great many newspapers are practically *owned* by advertisers; however, very few advertisers realize they have this clout.

If you're one of those people who agonizes over writing a simple letter, there's hope for you. *Power Real Estate Letters* (Real Estate Education Company, Chicago) includes a section on press releases, many of which can be quickly adapted to meet the majority of your needs (figure 8.1). The following are some possible topics for press releases:

- *Historical Information.* If a former owner was a significant local historical figure, this could be the basis of an article written on a new listing or property sold. The background of an old building either listed for sale or sold also makes an interesting press release. You could even write a historical piece about a new subdivision, such as the following: "Part of the original homestead of Thomas Kiley, who received the land from the U.S. Government in 1836, and has remained in the Kiley family for more than 100 years." History can also add a cachet to property. Finding historical data can be as easy as checking the abstract on the property or asking one of your local title companies for the chain of title. A discussion with a local historian should give you plenty of ammunition for a number of press releases. By checking local directories, you may find information on local descendants of early owners who can be quoted or included in photos for press releases. They may even have early photos you can use. An advantage of this historical type of press release is it may be published as a feature article in prime sections of the paper instead of with other releases in the real estate section.

- *Interesting Buyer or Seller.* When members of local society buy or sell, this is a newsworthy event. Besides a press release, you should also contact a local society columnist. Mentioning names can produce significant benefits, as there are always people who try to emulate those they consider the "in society." Then there are buyers with interesting or prestigious positions who are good for a feature article, especially if they are new to the community. New owners of local businesses are always newsworthy.

- *Significant Sales and Listings.* A large or expensive property listed for sale or sold should be covered with a press release.

- *News.* Ground-breaking ceremonies always make the news, but you can increase the newsworthiness of this type of story by photographing local politicians at the site. You will not have any trouble getting politicians for a photo opportunity. Also include floor plans with your press release and, if available, renderings of how the project will look.

- *Numbers.* The first sale in a new subdivision or the 100th sale are ideal press release subjects. Include discussions about the projects and buyers in these releases; the reasons they chose your subdivision is really a testimonial under the guise of a press release.

- *Your Office.* A new branch office or reaching a goal of $10,000,000 in sales or 100 transactions are excellent subjects for press releases.

- *Your Personnel.* Newly hired personnel can be the subject of a press release covering their work, background and families. Also, achievements such as "salesperson of the month" member of a *$1 million club,* or a new job title, such as *director of Subdivision Sales.*

Sample press releases are featured in figure 8.1.

FIGURE 8.1 Sample Press Releases

[*Henry Gibbs*] joins [*Clyde Realty*]

[*Thomas Flynn*], [*General Manager*] of [*Clyde Realty*], announced that [*Mr. Henry Gibbs*] recently joined the firm as a [*sales associate*] [*associate broker*]. [*Mr. Gibbs*] will be involved with [*home sales, primarily in the West Valley*].

[*Mrs. Gibbs*] is [*a graduate of Syracuse University and spent 12 years as a food broker in Chicago*]. [*He*] obtained [*his*] real estate license [*two years ago, and was previously associated with Boniface Construction Company, selling new homes in the Bellwood Heights development*]. [*Mr. Gibbs is a member of Thunderbird Country Club and resides in Bellwood Heights with his wife Eileen and their two daughters.*]

NOTE: *Send photo with all personnel press releases.*

NEWSLETTERS

Many firms buy monthly commercial newsletters to use as farming tools. The newsletters, printed with the firm's name, include several local articles on the front page and are supplied by the broker. The rest of the newsletter is "boilerplate" material also printed in many other newsletters. This material includes articles on types of mortgages, real estate trends, etc. However, these commercial types of newsletters are often trashed without being read.

If your market area is primarily a large, homogeneous subdivision or mobile home park, a personal newsletter makes sense. A personal newsletter could be your single most effective tool to make your firm dominant in its market area. An effective newsletter should be one that is sought after and read. To achieve this goal, it must contain information in which readers would be interested, such as:

- Free "want ad" section for items less than $1,000
- News from religious and secular organizations
- Local club meeting schedules
- Monthly resident profile

FIGURE 8.1   Sample Press Releases (continued)

New Project—[*Woodlake Village*]

[*Wilson Developers*] held their official ground breaking for the new [*122 single-family home Woodlake Village development*] on [*Wednesday, March 1st*]. Located [*on the northwest corner of Dunn Road and Woodlake Parkway*], the [*three-and four-bedroom family homes*] will feature [*up to 2,400 square feet. All homes will have three-car garages, tile roofs and eurostyle kitchens*].

[*Peggy Wilson*], the project sales coordinator for [*Clyde Realty*], the exclusive sales agent for [*Woodlake Village*], has indicated that the choice location coupled with moderate prices, starting at [*$122,500*] with [*10 percent*] financing, has already created an exceptional word-of-mouth interest in the development. According to [*Peggy Wilson*], the early reservations have been primarily from professionals in the real estate and construction industries.

NOTE: *For ground-breaking ceremonies, consider including a captioned photograph with local civic leaders and a builder representative as well as an agent of your firm.*

- News about residents, such as a 50th wedding anniversary
- Sales activity and information on new neighbors
- Special activities such as Little League, etc.

In addition, your newsletter could have a back page of display and classified ads on properties available through your office. Also, you could profile one of your salespersons each month and include articles on the local market, interest trends, etc. With a computer, laser printer and a desktop publishing program, you will be able to provide your local printer with quality camera-ready copy. Newsletters can be distributed to residents, used as mailing enclosures with inquiries from outside the area, supplied to the chamber of commerce and used as a valuable tool in a listing presentation.

Some firms assign a local resident as editor of their paper. He or she gains community status and is responsible for all but one or two pages of a four- or eight-page newsletter. One firm uses a nonpaid editor and provides secretarial help, a desk and

FIGURE 8.1   Sample Press Releases (continued)

[Retired Banker Chooses Meadowbrook]

Mr. and Mrs. [*Angus McCook*] have recently purchased [*a new home on Clancy Lane in Meadowbrook*]. [*Mr. McCook was active in banking for 40 years, having started as a teller with the Midvale Bank and rising to the presidency of the Newport Banking Group, one of the largest bank holding companies in the state.*]

[*Mr. and Mrs. McCook*] indicated they were attracted to Meadowbrook because of the [*choice of several outstanding golf courses and the general country atmosphere, close to the amenities of urban life*]. The purchase was arranged through the [*Meadowbrook office of Clyde Realty*].

NOTE: *A press release on a buyer is appropriate when the buyer has a distinguished or interesting background. Photos with captions should be included.*

business cards. The firm operates in a retirement area and sells ads to other local businesses, which pays for the printing costs.

LISTING PRESENTATION BOOKS

The effectiveness of a salesperson's listing presentation will be increased with the use of a listing presentation book. The book is generally separated into two distinct areas, "Why List?" and "Why Us?" The book would contain artwork and written explanations to go along with the salesperson's verbal presentation. It should also include sheets on the following:

- Why most people use real estate professionals
- What type of person is attracted to a For Sale By Owner sign
- Why most motivated buyers contact real estate agents
- Who really saves when the owner sells without an agent
- Problems of owner sales
- Why most For Sale By Owner signs are replaced by agent signs

FIGURE 8.1   Sample Press Releases (continued)

First Sale Made at [*English Village*]

[*Clyde Realty*], the exclusive sales agent for [*English Village*], has announced that [*Dr. and Mrs. Timothy Marks*] are the first home purchasers in [*the exclusive enclave of 16 estate homes in Bellwood*].

The [*Marks*] chose a [*3,600 square foot English country design*]. According to [*Dr. Marks*], they decided on [*English Village*] because of [*the huge lots, views, quality of design and construction as well as the country ambiance, which is so important with four small children*].

[*Currently three of the estate homes are under construction with the Marks' home scheduled for completion by August.*]

NOTE: *For a press release that provides information about a purchaser, be certain to obtain permission from the purchaser.*

In addition to publicity about your firm, a press release such as this one significantly reduces the possibility the purchaser will attempt to avoid the purchase closing.

The "Why Us?" portion should include the following:

- Information on the salesperson
- Information on your firm
- Advantages of a [small] [large] firm
- Information on MLS
- Press releases about you and/or your firm
- Photographs of homes with your Sold signs
- Letters of recommendations from owners (Testimonials)

The listing presentation book is pure advertising. It sets forth the advantage of having a professional sell your home, and follows through by showing your firm to be a professional fulfilling the owner's needs.

For a mock-up of a listing presentation book, see *Power Real Estate Listing,* 2nd edition (Real Estate Education Company).

FIGURE 8.1   Sample Press Releases (continued)

New [*Sales Manager*]

[*Henry Clyde, President of Clyde Realty*] has announced that [*Janet Jones*] has been appointed [*sales manager*] of [*Clyde Realty*].

[*Ms. Jones*] brings a wealth of experience to the position. [*She*] was formerly associated with [*Smith Realty*] as [*assistant sales manager*]. [*Ms. Jones*] has had more that [*eight*] years' experience in [*sales*] [*real estate sales*]. [*Ms. Jones*] has been with [*Clyde Realty*] for [*four years*]. [*Ms. Jones has received numerous honors, including membership in the prestigious Clyde Realty Million Dollar Roundtable.*] [*Ms. Jones received her bachelor's degree in business from Yale University.*] [*Ms. Jones attended New York University.*] [*She*] lives with [*her*] family in [*Midvale Heights*]. [*She has two children, John, nine years old, and Tammy, six.*] [*Her husband*] [*teaches English at South High School*]. [*Ms. Jones*] is active in [*Soroptimists and is an assistant girl scout leader*].

Source: *Power Real Estate Letters.* Copyright 1990, Dearborn Financial Publishing, Inc., Chicago.

PROPERTY BRIEFS

A property brief is usually a one-page flier that sells the virtues of one particular property. Property briefs should be prepared for every listing as soon as you have taken the listing. The brief should include a photo or drawing of the property.

If a photo is used it must have sharp contrasts so it reproduces well. Chances are it will need to be professionally retouched for reproduction purposes to make the property stand out.

A pen-and-ink drawing will reproduce far better than a photograph. Pen-and-ink drawings can convey a quality image that a photo often can't. There are a number of artists who specialize in these drawings, which are generally made by tracing over a photograph. A commercial artist experienced in this technique can produce a drawing in about a half-hour. The drawing can also be used in newspaper advertising.

One firm that uses pen and ink drawings for property briefs has the artist sign the originals. They then frame the original and present it to the buyer as a house-warming gift.

Because the property brief is simply an expanded advertisement, the same rules apply as for writing a good ad. However, for a property brief you don't have to be as limited as to space—*more* is generally better.

Your property brief should be loaded with descriptive adjectives. Remember, sell the benefits. For income property you could include a pro forma statement on the reverse side.

There are a number of great computer programs for preparing property briefs, such as Page Maker by Aldus Corporation, for both Macintosh and IBM computers. You might also want to consider The New Printshop program by Broderbund Software if you own an IBM or IBM-compatible computer.

A laser printer will give you excellent copy. You can then add any quality photograph, drawing or applicable clip art to your copy. You can also use a scanner to spice up your work. A scanner can "read" visual materials and transform them into computer files at almost any size you desire. Quality copies of artwork and photographs can then be produced on your printer.

Having your property brief prepared as soon as the listing is taken, will help you make it available to other agents for the caravan visit. Copies of the property brief should also be left at the property with a "take one" card for visitors to the property. They also should be supplied to other offices and salespeople active in the property's area. Property briefs can also be sent to persons outside the area who inquire as to properties.

When salespersons show a number of properties to prospective buyers, they become confused as to which property is which. Property briefs will alleviate this confusion and give buyers something to take with them to consider, so the property brief acts as a self-selling tool, even after the showing.

Producing quality property briefs is a significant selling tool in obtaining listings. Some agents actually prepare a sample property brief to show owners when they make their listing presentation.

It is possible to come up with a very impressive full-color property brief with the new color reproduction machines. The same color effect can be obtained by pasting a color photo of the property on the brief.

Figure 8.2 is an example of a property brief used by a Maryland multiple listing service. Notice how the line drawing presents a quality image.

DOOR HANGERS

If you actively farm for listings, you know the most effective method is face-to-face contact. In other words, you must go to the prospect's front door. You also know that with two-income families there is often no one home to answer the door, so rather than waste your time you place your business card in the door or use a door hanger. The door hanger, attached to the door handle, is a more visible and effective message for direct results than the usual institutional message of a business card. Consider using a call for help—a message aimed at finding a home for a real prospective buyer (figure 8.3). These types of door hangers have a short but useful life and must be printed up especially for specific buyers. Considering the value of your time and the possible benefits, they are well worth it.

Use real needs of a prospective buyer. A side benefit of this approach is that buyers will feel obligated to work with you, hopefully on an exclusive basis, because they see the effort you have expended on their behalf.

You want the prospective buyers to appear to be people the neighbors would like to know and assist. If there is a strong reason for neighborhood preference, include this in the copy. Door hangers are made of light card stock so part of it can be perforated and used as a tear-off business card.

While not as effective as a direct cry for help for a particular person, the door hanger in figure 8.4 is designed to appeal to a homeowner's avarice.

SPECIALTY ITEMS

Specialty items differ from premiums. Premiums must be earned, while specialty items are given "without obligation." One use is in door-to-door canvassing. Once you give homeowners something, they feel obligated to listen to you—at least for a few moments. Freebies are also given out at an open house or as Christmas gifts (see "Christmas Cards," section, this chapter). Some agents give them away at public speaking engagements.

In choosing your specialty gift, you not only want it to be inexpensive, but also one that will not be thrown away. As an example, no one throws out a ruler or yardstick. Unfortunately, these end up in drawers or closets. A better specialty gift is one that is likely to be seen daily. A refrigerator magnet, especially one with a clip attachment, will likely be used. Other specialty gift ideas include memo pads, calendars, coin purses, and key rings. Of course, the gift must have your name, telephone

FIGURE 8.2   Property Brief

Source: Central Maryland Multiple Listing Service, Inc. Adapted with permission.

FIGURE 8.3   Door Hanger Designed as a Call for Help

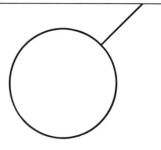

Can You Help
A Future
Neighbor?

We are trying to find a 3BR home in your neighborhood for a young family with a seven-year-old son and four-year-old daughter. The parents, engineers, are being transferred to the area. They very much want to be in the Midvale School District because of its fine reputation. If you know of anyone planning to relocate, we would appreciate your help.

Tom Brown
Clyde Realty   555-8200
                                              Eve: 555-9610

Tom Brown
Associate Broker
Clyde Realty
912 Sun Plaza
Midvale 92413

Eve: 555-9610   **555-8200**

FIGURE 8.4 Door Hanger Designed To Appeal to a Homeowner's Finances

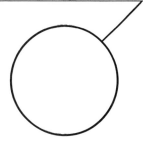

Want To Know What Your Home Is Worth?

Because of market changes, your home could be worth far more than you imagined.

Call me today for a

Free, No Obligation

computer-generated competitive market analysis, which will indicate just what your home is worth in today's marketplace.
(Of course when you consider selling, we hope you will remember Clyde Realty.)

Tom Brown
Eve: 555-9610   555-8200

Tom Brown
Associate Broker
Clyde Realty
912 Sun Plaza
Midvale 92413

Eve: 555-9610   **555-8200**

FIGURE 8.5 Sample Program Book Advertisements

A Real Estate Career?

Like to work at your own pace? Do you like to help people? Do you like to search for solutions? Or, are you simply tired of nothing to do. A career in real estate could be the answer. Want to learn more? Call me so we can personally explore your future.

[Logo]   **Tom Higgins, General Manager**
Clyde Realty   **555-8200**

We Want a Few Good Women (and Men)

No, we are not recruiting for the Marines. We are looking for socially concerned citizens who want to help others in fulfilling their needs. Attributes we regard as essential are honesty and regard for others. Age is not a selection factor. We are proud of our staff and if you feel you meet our qualifications, I would like to show you how you can become a part of this team.

Tom Clyde
  [Logo]
Clyde Realty   **555-8200**

number and possibly your firm's logo on it. If possible, choose colors that tie in with colors of the firm's signs. An informative booklet on choosing a new home could be an excellent giveaway item at open houses.

CHARITY ADS AND SPONSORSHIPS

As a general rule, the cost of ads in program books, organizational books, etc., does not justify the benefits received. People who sell program booklet advertising first check to see who previously purchased ads for other similar programs. Once you buy one ad, you can expect to be bombarded by other organizations happy to place you in the awkward position of, "You gave them an ad, what do you have against our organization?"

There are times, however, when you can't say no! to an ad request. This explains why some program ads simply say "compliments of a friend." This is done to avoid pressure to buy additional advertising in similar publications. Normally, when a person does buy an ad in a program book, they either reproduce their business card or simply use their firm name. They receive very little institutional value from such an ad. It is, however, possible to increase the benefit of these charity ads. Before and during events, people read through program books, sometimes out of lack of anything else to do while waiting for the event to begin.

Figure 8.5 features several ads that not only give you institutional advantage, but direct benefits as well.

In addition to advertising for salespersons, you can place a classified or display ad for a particular property. Wherever possible your ad should be tailored to its likely readers. As an example, a horse-show program booklet could advertise a property zoned for horses or with horse facilities. Such readers likely have above-average incomes, so you could alternately advertise an investment property.

Charity advertisements are not cost-effective; nevertheless, keep in mind it need not mean dollars wasted. If you are going to invest in such an ad, maximize its effectiveness.

Many organizations are not what they appear to be. Some are actually formed simply to sell ads. As an example, ad solicitation to help a certain organization may not aid the group you think you are benefiting. Instead, it might be an organization whose major purpose is to aid the promoter. Therefore, we advise you not to buy ads over the telephone unless you personally know the caller or organization. Ask for information about the organization in writing. Chances are, you won't get a reply if the call is not legitimate.

Team sponsorships are usually not effective advertising for real estate firms although there are exceptions (see Chapter 10). Unless you own a combination real estate office and pizzeria, having your firm name emblazoned on the back of a team's shirts won't necessarily increase your business. However, if your child is a member of Little League and your spouse reminds you of the need of a team sponsor, discretion may indeed be the better part of valor.

CHRISTMAS AND HOLIDAY CARDS

Chances are your office is going to send out Christmas or other holiday cards. If so, you will want to get maximum benefit. Avoid overly religious cards and messages unless all the recipients have similar beliefs as those reflected in your cards. While you don't want to take Christ out of the recipient's Christmas celebration, you might consider a simple, "Season's Greetings and Best Wishes for a Healthy and Happy New Year."

Refrain from using commerical cards. A card with a photo of your entire staff would be better. A personal touch could include an additional handwritten note to each recipient. Salespersons should also personalize their office cards with a personal note and photo of their family and, yes, the family pets. Salespeople should send cards to the parents of their small children's friends, neighbors within a one-block radius of their home, friends, members of religious and social organizations to which they belong, and current buyers and sellers and former clients with whom they have worked. Christmas or holiday cards are just about your only chance to sell yourself as a caring person who has a high regard for family values. People like to work with this type of person in solving their real estate problems.

Instead of Christmas cards, some firms send out booklets with the words to Christmas carols (a caroler's handbook). An advantage to this approach over regular Christmas cards is they are more likely to be retained.

9 Special Promotions

Besides your ordinary use of the various media available, a number of special techniques and marketing plans are available for special purposes.

COUPONS AND CONTESTS

We are a nation of coupon-clippers. Should you doubt this, get in line at any supermarket when you're in a hurry. We have cents-off, two-for-one and even free gift coupons. While widely used by retail merchandisers and service providers, coupons can also be effectively used in real estate.

Coupons tend to increase the effectiveness of special offers. A free competitive market analysis coupon can be used as a mailing piece, newspaper ad or even on a door hanger. Coupons can also be used in open house ads as deposits for a prize drawing. Another example would be a coupon offering one month's free rent to quickly fill a new rental project, rather than simply offering one month free rent. Incidentally, the one month free rent should be the 12th month in a one-year lease, not the first month.

Some sample coupons for special items with a home purchase are shown in figure 9.1.

Using the coupon approach in classified columns will make your ads stand out from others. The coupon in figure 9.2 really is not a coupon.

Some developments where likely buyers travel from some distance away have successfully included coupons in their ads good, when validated at the development, for free gas at a station close to the development. Because the service station benefits, as the customer usually buys more than the minimum amount, a validated five-dollar coupon exchanged for gas may only cost the developer four dollars.

An approach to be used when you have a number of open house events in an area is to offer visitors a chance at a

FIGURE 9.1   Sample Coupon and Lottery Ticket

Free
$3,000

In Household Appliances

Free: 22 Ft. Whirlpool side-by-side refrigerator
with in-door ice maker
Free: Hotpoint self-cleaning oven and range
Free: Maytag washer and dryer
with every new home purchased during

Willow Woods
(1 block west of Highway 17 at Exit 223)
Grand Opening
Family Homes from $124,500–$139,600
with FHA and VA Financing Available

Clyde Realty   **555-8200**

This relatively small display ad is very effective based on cost. The ad could also be tailored for classified columns, or as a cut-out coupon with a larger display ad for the development. Offering appliances free rather than including them with the house gives you a strong advertising hook.

Free—Win $10,000,000

or more

During our Grand Opening every adult or visitor to Hillsdale Estates will receive a California lottery ticket absolutely free.

You may be the lucky winner.

The above coupon ad was designed to be included within a grand opening ad; however, it could be expanded on to stand by itself. With the lottery mania today, giving away lottery tickets is effective yet far less expensive and less annoying than giving free food or other gifts.

FIGURE 9.2 Classified "Coupon" for Intangible Benefits of Home Ownership

---

Good for One Free Hug

from your family when they see this perfect 3 BR, 2 Bath Williamsburg Colonial set beneath giant oaks amidst flowering shrubs on an estate size lot in Westlake. You'll love the lazy-day screened veranda, paneled dining room, barbecue-perfect patio and gleaming hardwood floors. Everything on your wish list for only $169,500.

Clyde Realty   555-8200

FIGURE 9.3 "Bingo" Open House Tour Notice

"Bingo" Open House Tour
1–4 P.M. Today
You Can Be the Big Winner!

B   3BR, 2 bath colonial set amidst towering maples.
     1820 Woodside Lane   = $127,800

I   4BR American bungalow with a huge fenced yard your children will love.
     4237 Morningside   = $112,500

N   3BR, 1½ bath brick split ranch with huge recreation room.
     1643 Jacob's Trail   = $97,500

G   2BR + Den, 1¾ bath Cape Cod in a storybook wooded setting.
     1511 Hillside Lane   = $109,500

O   3BR, 2 bath contemporary with soaring ceilings and walls of glass.
     1521 Woodside Terrace   = $121,500

You will receive a sealed letter at each home

5 letters spelling *Bingo* = 19" Color TV
4 of the letters of *Bingo* = 5" B & W TV
3 of the letters of *Bingo* = Transistor Radio
2 of the letters of *Bingo* = Dodgers Baseball Cap

Clyde Realty   **555-8200**

---

prize which requires them to view a group of homes (figure 9.3).

Bingo or lotto open house tours can be used as weekly events if you have a good-size inventory. The beauty of bingo tours is you will probably have house seekers for the entire afternoon touring all the homes, especially after receiving a winning letter at their first stop. Besides being in the same general area, tour homes should all be within a 20 percent price range. A press release complete with a photo of a color TV winner will increase your bingo tour attendance.

A coloring contest for children with bicycles for prizes can be an effective model home attraction. Consider a drawing of the development or model home in your ad for children to color as a contest entry to be deposited at the sales office.

While not a coupon or contest, trading stamps were very popular at one time. They will likely be a marketing tool in the future if the cycle of interest theory holds true. About 20 years ago, many households collected stamps with almost religious zeal for use at gift redemption centers. At least one large brokerage firm offered trading stamps on home purchases. Not only did this increase traffic and sales, it increased listings as well, because the firm offered something that made a home owner's home more desirable. Strangely enough, many home purchases were influenced by the chance to earn several hundred dollars in *free* merchandise. The firm received positive publicity from a press release depicting one couple practically smothered with ribbons of trading stamps.

SUBDIVISION MARKETING

For a large development, you want a well-planned advertising campaign in place well before the grand opening. You want ads completed, signs ordered, and all elements ready to go. Because of construction problems, you should realize the dates might change.

Your ads should tie together so as not to appear disjointed. As an example, one subdivider started with advance ads telling people they couldn't buy a new ranch home in his new development for $128,500 until April 15th. His "Sorry, you will have to wait" approach created exceptional interest. After his grand opening, each of his ads featured a short testimonial from real buyers about why they purchased in his development. To get testimonial letters *all you need to do is ask.*

When marketing a number of properties for builders or developers, brokers tend to concentrate on display ads and ignore the classified columns. Classified ads, however, can be a valuable adjunct to display ads. While prospective buyers interested in viewing projects from models are attracted by display ads and project signs, buyers who were primarily interested in the resale market can be reached through classified ads. The classified ads in figure 9.4 can be used effectively in selling new development properties.

FIGURE 9.4 Classified Advertisements for Developments

Get in Line

with your money in hand if you want to become the owner of 1 of these last 4 brick, 3BR, 2½-bath town houses in Clydewood Estates. When these are gone, there won't be any more. Each unit has a huge 2-car garage (with room for a hobby shop), all appliances, ceramic-tiled kitchen floor, baths sheathed in marble, Jacuzzi tub in the master suite and all the model home features you dream of. They should sell out quickly at $164,500.

Clyde Realty   **476-8200**

Builder S.O.S.

We must sell 7 brand-new 3BR, 2-bath ranch homes on estate-sized lots in prestigious Westwood Hills by this weekend. All homes have full basements; 2-car, attached garages; quality carpets; hardwood trim; Eurostyle kitchens; covered rear patios; and front yard landscaping. Save thousands. It is first come, first served at $124,500.

Clyde Realty   **476-8200**

Source: *Simplified Classifieds—1001 Real Estate Ads That Sell.* Copyright 1990, Dearborn Financial Publishing, Inc., Chicago.

Choosing a name for a new development can help sales. A name that creates a desirable image, which owners will want to use when talking about their homes, will help to bring traffic to your models. Consider the following examples:

- Hidden Cove
- Mariner's Walk
- Nantucket Landing
- Oak Glen
- Spyglass Hill
- Waterford Village

The names of your model homes can also help you in your sales. They should be names that evoke a positive image. As an example, if the architecture was Spanish with a profusion of tile, models could be given such names as:

- The Majorca
- The Paloma
- The Seville

These names carry a romantic image of tile roofs and soft guitars. In fact, music can be used to carry out a theme. Soft Spanish music both outside and inside the models could help to carry out a positive mood and tie in with the Spanish theme.

The architect's name, even if not well known, can add prestige to a home. By stating that "This colonial home was designed by Stanford Evans Brown" in your ads as well as on the plaque with the model name, conveys to the prospective buyer that the house is special.

In your ads, state directions to new subdivisions clearly. Directional signs should be used on all major roads and intersections to direct traffic to the development. Use the same logo in your directional signs as in your ads. The color of your directional signs should be distinctive and uniform so prospective buyers can find your development among a multitude of signs. Larger developments should also consider billboards.

Don't place your signs on utility poles or private property, as they are likely to be removed by city officials. While local politicians may be able to get away with signs in these places, a real estate agent who does the same may not only lose the signs but could also be fined.

Flags and banners are especially important when your development is off a major road but can be seen from the road. Flags should be on higher standards so they can be seen.

Some developers use search lights for grand openings. This is generally a waste of money as new homes are seldom viewed after dark. A better approach is to tether several brightly colored, hot-air balloons at the development. Their sheer size is an attraction. They can usually be rented from private balloon owners at reasonable rates because hobbyists are often eager to show off their balloons.

One developer talked a local hot air balloon club into featuring a race starting at his new development during his grand opening. His only expense was a group of trophies. The event brought him over 1,000 visitors for the 10 A.M., Saturday morning race.

Skydivers are attention-getters. One developer contacted a skydiving club and had a skydiving competition as part of his grand opening event. He paid for the plane rental and the trophies. Before you plan such an event, however, make certain you have adequate liability insurance coverage.

Still another developer sponsored a 10K race that ended at his new developments, with the winner of the race breaking the ribbon for the grand opening. Proceeds from the event went to a local charity. Participants in the race all received T-shirts prominently displaying the name of the development and the charity. The developer received a lot of pre-race and post-race publicity from the race as well as community goodwill.

A simple and low-cost attraction is a large arch of party-type balloons filled with helium. The arch can be several hundred feet high and can be the entryway to the development (figure 9.5).

Many new developments offer food as an attraction to visit new developments. Besides being messy, the money spent offers

FIGURE 9.5 Archway of Balloons over Entry to Development

little long-term benefit. For less money, each visitor could receive a plastic sunshade (ideal for golfers) imprinted with the name of the development. For more money but still less than catering costs, a baseball cap carrying the name of your firm could be offered. While a hamburger and a coke will soon be forgotten, the caps and sunshades will continue to advertise your firm or development.

Another developer hires someone with an Easter Bunny costume at Easter and a Santa Claus costume for the Christmas holidays. He advertises free photographs of the children with the Easter Bunny or Santa. He gives a 5″ × 7″ photo, including a cardboard display frame, to the parents. Because the developer allows the photographer to sell 8″ × 10″ photos at $4.99 and other assorted size photos at $9.99 he doesn't have to pay the photographer. The developer using the free photos in his ads claims this is the most cost-effective premium he has ever used. For other promotional ideas, see "Coupons and Contests" section, this chapter.

You might want to have a pre-grand opening. You can use this as a charity fund-raiser. Black-tie events in some communities have been successful in generating excellent society coverage, which has helped the image of the development. The charity sells the tickets to the event and you underwrite food, beverage and music costs. While it is expensive, a fund raiser for an "in" charity can be worthwhile in total benefits received.

Always invite local real estate editors and columnists as well as society columnists to your grand openings. Be certain they are given VIP treatment. Make certain they are supplied with glossy photos (of the event and the development). You want them to view your project in the best possible light. This will increase the likelihood of all of your press releases being published as well as of obtaining newspaper staff coverage.

Grand opening ad costs can be shared. Even if manufacturers of key components do not offer Co-op advertising (and in a great many cases they do), suppliers, contractors and subcontractors can generally be induced to share in the cost of a large display ad or brochure that points out that their firm was responsible for some features such as kitchen cabinets, tile work, plumbing, electricity, appliances, air-conditioning, etc.

Obtain competitive bids on your printing. Some real estate firms take their work to a printer who then simply sends it on to another printer who is better equipped to handle the job, but charges a mark-up for services. Printing brokers can also place your printing order for you at a modest fee.

Hand-out materials must be provided to development visitors. Consider using a folder with separate flyers inside for each model. You can obtain color in your packet, as well as make it easier for viewers to review the material, by using different colored sheets for each model home. The fliers should have a pen-and-ink drawing of the model as well as a floor plan. It is best to set forth the price right on the flier rather than use a separate price sheet. This makes it easier for viewers to make decisions.

For a grand opening, the flier could hint that these are the initial prices and could be raised later. You can accomplish this with "grand opening price" or "price guaranteed until November 15th only."

All too often, developments leave out financing details in their handouts. Don't leave this to the salespeople. Include a financing sheet giving down payments and monthly payments for the homes using various available loans. Chances are that adjustable rate loans with a teaser rate are available so the low initial interest rate and monthly payment can be shown.

Your handout material might also include information on community services, schools, etc. Often, chamber of commerce material can be integrated into your handout material. Make certain that your business card is attached to all material generated by others. Every sheet in the packet must bear the name of your development, address and telephone number (often people visit several developments and mix up the material).

One way to make certain visitors to your development appreciate all of your standard features is to use signs in the model which identify the quality features and amenities that might otherwise be overlooked. Some developers use arrows with the signs. Example would be, "triple glazed windows," "solid hardwood cabinets," "Marble countertops," "Solid oak trim," "$600 electrical fixture allowance," "Whirlpool spa," "Choice of Berber or plush Stainmaster carpeting," "Maytag appliances included," "Lenox air-conditioning," etc.

If you are handling your first project, get professional photos of the opening and save copies of all your ads, then put the material together in a presentation book, film strip or video-tape. You can then promote your handling of the project to obtain representation from other developers on their planned projects.

The ad in figure 9.6 was part of a series of ads around "the lady of the lake" theme, which was used to attract interest in a quality development. While the lady of the lake was later pictured in gossamer-like attire against the background of the lake and mountains, the homes were not shown in these ads.

VISITOR PACKAGES

Vacation and retirement properties are often sold to buyers coming from other geographical areas. To increase the likelihood of a visit to a development, a number of brokers and developers have arranged visitor packages consisting of lodging, use of recreational facilities and even several meals. These induce buyers to visit a particular development as well as make them feel an obligation to the firm that supplied the visitor package. Some firms feature the visitor package in ads and mailings, while others send package information only to those who inquire about properties. Often, coupons are used in these mailings.

Some Florida brokers offer to pay air fares and lodging for visitors, but only if they buy through that broker. We believe this to be an unprofessional approach with a negative effect that outweighs the limited positive results. Many capable buyers are turned off by free packages due to the abusive sales tactics tied in with the free visitations practiced by time-share and land sales firms. A far better approach would be to charge for the package. In many cases broker's or developer's costs, above the fee charged, will actually be nominal if offered during other than peak periods. Charging for the package rather than offering it free will also get a higher rate of response from qualified buyers. Many people feel reluctant to accept a free package.

FIGURE 9.6   "Lady of the Lake" Promotion for Development

Have You
Seen Her Yet?

The Lady of The Lake

*Once you have seen where she lives
nothing else will ever look the same*

The Lady of the Lake

Irresistible Waterfront Homes

(619) 564-5407

Take I-10, exit Washington south. Lake La Quinta is located approximately ¼ mile past Hwy. 111 on Washington. Look for the signs.

Sales office open 10:00 a.m. to 5:00 p.m. daily.

Source: Roddan Public Relations Advertising. Reprinted with permission.

FIGURE 9.7   Special Package Offer

**Lake Air Estates
2 Nights—King-Size Suite
Paradise Lodge**

- Free cocktail party
- Free breakfast buffets
- Free tennis
- Half-price Golf—at the fabulous Los Rosas Country Club
- Free airport pickup

**Only $119 Per Couple
for this complete
visitor's package**

Call: **1-800-621-9626**
for your Reservation Confirmation

Rather than having a sense of obligation or being a "free-loader," by paying for the package they feel they are in control.

The flier in figure 9.7 can be mailed with property inquiries. Using the "800" number of the project sales office ensures immediate responses to the flier. Should there be a cocktail party, it should be held at the development or at a sales office, giving agents an opportunity to learn about buyers' needs and desires. Also, consider setting up the "offer" copy to appear as a coupon with a heavy border within the body of an advertisement.

OPEN HOUSE

Normally, classified ads are used to promote an open house (figure 9.8). Besides being inserted in the proper ad category, open house ads should also include the following:

- The fact that it is an open house
- The days and hours of the open house
- Address and directions so the viewer can readily locate the open house
- Price (special terms included if applicable)
- Desirable features that would customarily be included in any ad

---

FIGURE 9.8 Classified Ads for an Open House

Open House—
$189,500
1224 Midbury
12:00–4:00 P.M. Today
Bring Your Boots

The hammering has stopped, but the lawn and walks haven't been completed on this 3BR, 2-bath Carolina Traditional, so it could get muddy. The home is on an estate-sized lot and features spacious rooms, a real country kitchen with all the built-ins you can want, 2 fireplaces, a den or office with a private entry, a 3-car garage and a full basement awaiting your imagination. We're sorry the home still needs a few finishing touches, but it seems every home this builder builds is snapped up well before completion. At this price, this one will likely do the same. Follow the signs from the corner of Millbury and Westhaven.

Clyde Realty   **476-8200**

First Opening
Sat.–Sun., 1–4 P.M.
4218 Edgewater Circle
**(Follow the signs
from the corner of 1st
and Ocean View Drive.)**

This 3BR, 2-bath, cedar and stone beach home has an ocean view and is just steps from the sand with off-street parking for 3 cars. This definitely won't last at $249,500.

Clyde Realty   **476-8200**

Be sure to draw attention to the fact that a home is being offered or opened for the first time. This is important to many buyers who feel something must be wrong with any house that has been on the market for several months. Where parking is in critical supply, your ad should point out any extra parking.

Open To Sell
Sat.–Sun., 1–4 P.M.
3822 West 17th Street

This is a like-new, 3BR, 2-bath American Colonial in a premier location. The home includes an attached, double garage; full basement; and every amenity you dream of.

$99,500–
$10,000 Down

Clyde Realty   **476-8200**

Other headings are "open for appreciation," "first opening," or simply "open house."

Open Today
1–4 P.M.—$97,500
Will Be Sold
by Tomorrow
1212 W. Burnham
**(1 block
west of Kilbourn)**

The owner of this 3BR, 2-bath, Tennessee stone ranch has priced this fine residence for immediate sale. Set on an estate-sized lot in a much sought-after community of fine homes, special features include a massive fireplace in the huge living area, a separate formal dining room, a cozy den and a full basement completely finished with recreation room and workroom. There is even a perfect spot for a photographer's darkroom. Better be the first in line.

Clyde Realty   **476-8200**

FIGURE 9.9   Distinctive Open-House Directional Signs

OPEN HOUSE

LOW DOWN

O
P
E
N

Strips for particularly desirable
features can be added to the sign

If you polled open house visitors, many would say they had not seen the ads. They were looking around the area or were responding to another agent's ad when they discovered your open house.

Because many open house visitors are the result of direct visual impressions, you want the visual impressions to be as noticeable as possible. Some brokers use standard rectangular signs with "open house" or "open house" with an arrow directing persons to the property.

If you are directing people to an open house from other streets and there are competing signs, consider distinctive signs as to color and shape (figure 9.9); large arrows on metal stakes work well.

Ask the owners when you wish to put a sign directing traffic on their property. Most owners will give their permission if you ask properly: Introduce yourself, give them a business card and ask permission, letting the owner know how long your sign will be on the property. If you don't ask permission, chances are your sign will disappear for good.

Some brokers tie colorful helium balloons on all of their signs. It makes it easier to find a project among competing directional signs. Good directionals will actually capture prospects looking for other homes or projects.

A California sales agent has his own large helium blimp with "Open House" printed on it (figure 9.10). He tethers the blimp to the open house. The same agent has a bubble machine blowing thousands of large bubbles in the air. It is a strong attraction for family housing. Besides making the house stand out, it attracts children, which sets a proper sales atmosphere.

Large open house banners and pendants are generally associated with project sales, but they can also be used at open

FIGURE 9.10 Novelty Blimp To Promote Open House

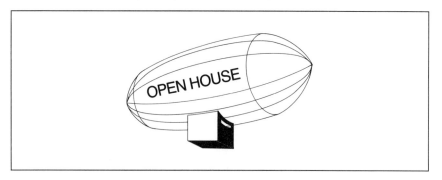

FIGURE 9.11 Motion Sign To Promote Open House

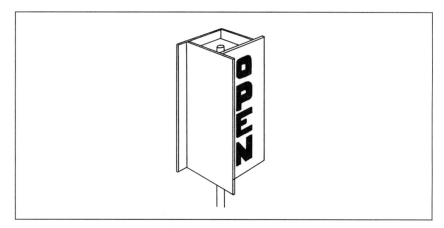

houses. They are available ready made from real estate office supply firms at a fraction of the cost for custom banners. There are commercially available motion signs that use color and motion to attract attention (figure 9.11). These are placed on the property.

If the open house is in an area with strict sign ordinances, you might have to pay a fee just to put up an open house sign. Even then, you could be limited to size and a drab color. Some agents have found ways to get around these limitations by placing large magnetic "open house" signs on their cars and parking them in the driveway toward the street for greatest visibility. A brightly colored mobile office, especially when it reads "open house—office" can also be effective (see "Traveling Ads" section, Chapter 6).

An open house is an opportunity to interest prospective buyers not only in the home open for viewing, but in other homes as well. You should have property briefs (see Chapter 8) available for other properties as well as a property brief on the property being shown. If viewers have a property brief, they are less likely to confuse your property with others when they may be viewing multiple properties.

People attracted to an open house by an ad are generally able and willing to buy a home priced higher than the house they are viewing. It is really a bargain syndrome where the prospective buyers hope to find what they want for less than they are willing to pay.

On the other hand, visitors to an open house who respond because of the sign out front, or who followed your arrow signs, are coming into the house blind as to price. Again, they are looking for bargains. They are hoping to find a home better than any they have seen so far, in an area they consider desirable, at a price they can afford. These people are often looking at homes listed 10 to 20 percent above their financial abilities.

Because of these two divergent groups, you should have property briefs available at the open house for homes priced around 15 percent above and below the open house property. You should also include property briefs for homes within the price range of the open house.

Your office should prepare a map showing clearly how viewers can locate each open house. You should include a paragraph about each house, which is written like a classified ad to intrigue the reader. In this manner, you will create traffic for each of your other open houses. This map should be given to every visitor before they leave.

For multiple open houses, consider the bingo tour discussed in Chapter 9. If you can get a model home listing in a "parade of homes" or similar home tour of new homes, this listing can be very valuable and sell not only the listed home. You should have adequate staff for a parade of homes so you can get the name and telephone number of every visitor and give out handout material about your firm as well as the house visited. Because of the traffic some parade of homes generate, some brokers offer builders extremely attractive agreements to have an opportunity at this traffic.

You want every open house visitor to sign a register. In order to increase the likelihood of their completing a registration card, you should have a reason such as "To evaluate the effectiveness of our advertising." Real estate office supply firms carry open house registration cards, which can be used to evaluate the advertising yet provide all the data you want.

You can treat open houses much like a model home with the use of signs pointing out features of the home. Signs could point out things such as, "Central alarm system," "220 elec + gas," "Maytag appliances," "6 inches of wall insulation," etc. Packets of assorted signs are available from several sources, including Superior Real Estate Supply, 301 Osborn Road, #1000, Phoenix, AZ 85013, or you can call 1-800-234-0592; and Sanzo Specialties, Inc., P.O. Box 68, Endicott, NY 13760, or call 1-800-222-4041. These are two of the larger real estate supply firms. You will find many items of interest in their catalogs.

OPEN HOUSE FOR AGENTS

In large metropolitan areas, agents can only caravan a small percentage of new listings, but the greater exposure you give a property, the better the chance for a quick sale. Everyone loves a party and agents are no exception. Champagne and hors d'oeuvres or wine and cheese on a Friday afternoon is a welcome relief for many agents. Open house for agents should have a "hook" to bring them in, such as a door prize, a special "spiff" to sell a property, or both. Spiff money or push money is a little "something extra" you give a salesperson for a sale or listing.

One successful broker purchased a slot machine, had it modified to accept tokens, and supplied tokens to the agents to play the slot machine. The machine paid off in more tokens, which could be redeemed for gifts. Gifts ranged from small calculators to car phones and vacation trips.

Owners love agent open houses because they show the owners you are doing everything possible to sell their property. Fliers used to promote agent open houses should be part of your listing presentation book. Properties chosen for agent open houses should be fairly priced or you won't get many agents to come to a second open house. For a builder with several homes or condominiums, an agent open house is a natural.

The flier in figure 9.12 is a sample of the advertising you could use for your agent open house. The flier could be posted at board offices, distributed at board meetings and mailed to other offices. You should also call agents who are particularly active in the area or sale of the particular type of property and invite them personally.

FIGURE 9.12 Flier for Agent Open House

Source: Copyright 1982, Central Maryland Multiple Listing Service, Inc. Adapted with permission.

10 Putting It All Together

In developing your own advertising plan, first consider your goals, including the market you seek and stature you plan to obtain within that market. Then develop an advertising budget based on anticipated company commissions (company dollar). Decide on the percentage of your company dollar to be allocated for advertising. This will depend upon your particular market costs for media, the market you aim at and particular goals. After you have developed your budget, you must then allocate dollars (or percentages) to various media based on expected benefits versus cost and your needs. Your advertising plan is not cast in stone. Changes in economics, in local media costs, in office commissions received and in your goals will necessitate varying your advertising plan.

The following checklist will alert you to deficiencies, in your present advertising and will help you develop a future advertising program. This checklist should be completed after you have fully reviewed the preceding nine chapters.

ANALYZING MY ADVERTISING

Does your firm have a logo?   ☐ Yes   ☐ No

Does the logo tie in with all your visual advertising?   ☐ Yes   ☐ No

Do you and all your employees wear name tags on a regular basis?   ☐ Yes   ☐ No

Are your business cards distinctive?   ☐ Yes   ☐ No

Are home telephone numbers on your business cards?   ☐ Yes   ☐ No

Do your business cards tie in with your signs and advertising?   ☐ Yes   ☐ No

Do your present business cards include recent photographs?   ☐ Yes   ☐ No

Do you and/or all employees have home telephone answering machines?   ☐ Yes   ☐ No

Have you reviewed message machine messages for effectiveness?   ☐ Yes   ☐ No

Do you and your employees have and regularly use magnetic car signs?   ☐ Yes   ☐ No

If yes, do the car signs tie in with the color and logo used in your other advertising?   ☐ Yes   ☐ No

Would rear car signs be appropriate for your vehicle and employees vehicles?   ☐ Yes   ☐ No

Are you available to speak before civic groups on real estate matters of interest?   ☐ Yes   ☐ No

Do your local papers currently have a regular local real estate column?   ☐ Yes   ☐ No

Have you ever personally talked to real estate editors of local papers as to a real estate column or press release?   ☐ Yes   ☐ No

Does your office sign stand out?   ☐ Yes   ☐ No

If not, what if anything, could be done to improve the sign?_____

_____

Is it possible for you to have a lighted message marquee or outside lighted bulletin board?   ☐ Yes   ☐ No

If so, do you have one?   ☐ Yes   ☐ No

Would it be possible to have your firm name as the name of the building you occupy?   ☐ Yes   ☐ No

Does your office area have significant foot traffic?   ☐ Yes   ☐ No

Do you have ground-floor window areas suitable for display?   ☐ Yes   ☐ No

Do you currently have window displays of your inventory?   ☐ Yes   ☐ No

Do you have a place where an electronic moving message would be effective?   ☐ Yes   ☐ No

What could you do to improve your window displays?_____

_____

Can a passerby clearly see into your office?   ☐ Yes   ☐ No

Is your office well lighted?   ☐ Yes   ☐ No

Is your office parking area well lighted?   ☐ Yes   ☐ No

What kind of impression does the exterior appearance of your firm give?_____

_____

Does your office waiting room area have literature that sells your firm or inventory?
☐ Yes   ☐ No

Do the furnishings of your office convey integrity and competence?   ☐ Yes   ☐ No

Does your attire and the dress of your coworkers indicate professionalism?   ☐ Yes   ☐ No

Does your office do a significant amount of advertising outside your geographical area?
☐ Yes   ☐ No

Do you have an "800" telephone number?   ☐ Yes   ☐ No

Does your office have promotional sales events for employees?   ☐ Yes   ☐ No

If yes, how could they be improved? _____

_____

Are you currently recruiting the quantity and quality of salesperson you desire?   ☐ Yes   ☐ No

Do you use ads for recruitment?   ☐ Yes   ☐ No

How could they be improved? _____

_____

Do you use word-of-mouth staff recruitment?   ☐ Yes   ☐ No

If not, why not? _____

_____

Will one glance at one of your for sale signs tell a local resident the sign is your firm's?
☐ Yes   ☐ No

If not, why not? _____

_____

Do you use sign strips for evening numbers and special features?   ☐ Yes   ☐ No

Have you considered "talking signs"?   ☐ Yes   ☐ No

Do you use special For Sale signs for land or commercial property?   ☐ Yes   ☐ No

What could be done to have more effective signage? _____

_____

Who writes your classified ads? _____

How much time, on average, is devoted to writing each ad? _____

Are classified ads generally prepared just before the advertising deadline?   ☐ Yes   ☐ No

In writing your classified ads, do you consider avoiding widows?   ☐ Yes   ☐ No

If a property has a particularly desirable feature or location, is it used in the ad heading?
☐ Yes   ☐ No

If not, why not? _____

_____

Where do ad ideas customarily come from? _____

Are multiple ads prepared for each property appealing to different groups of likely buyers?
☐ Yes   ☐ No

Do you use the same classified ad for a property in more than one paper?   ☐ Yes   ☐ No

How many days to you customarily insert a classified ad? _____ days

Is the same ad again used at a later date?   ☐ Yes   ☐ No

Is price generally included in your classified ads?   ☐ Yes   ☐ No

Is your logo included in your classified ads?   ☐ Yes   ☐ No

Do you use slugs for accent in your ads?   ☐ Yes   ☐ No

Do your classified ads stand out in a positive manner from your competition's?   ☐ Yes   ☐ No

How would you rate your classified ads in comparison with ads of your competitors? _____

_____

What could you do to improve your classified ads? _____

_____

Do you regularly check newspapers to see if your ads were typeset properly and inserted on the proper days and in the correct categories?   ☐ Yes   ☐ No

Do you customarily use display ads?   ☐ Yes   ☐ No

For what purpose? _____

_____

For what type of property? _____

_____

Do you market new subdivisions?   ☐ Yes   ☐ No

Do you market commercial property?   ☐ Yes   ☐ No

Do you market luxury homes?   ☐ Yes   ☐ No

If you are currently using display ads, who prepares these ads? _____

Do your display ads stand out from your competitor's ads?   ☐ Yes   ☐ No

Do you use photos or drawings in your display ads?   ☐ Yes   ☐ No

Do the photos or drawings reproduce well?   ☐ Yes   ☐ No

Do your display ads appear crowded?   ☐ Yes   ☐ No

Do you use long sentences in your ad copy?   ☐ Yes   ☐ No

Do you use capital letters for the entire heading or ad?   ☐ Yes   ☐ No

Do your display ads include your logo?   ☐ Yes   ☐ No

Do your ad headings grab the reader's attention? ☐ Yes ☐ No

Do you have anyone review your display ads for clarity? ☐ Yes ☐ No

Have you used testimonials in your display ads? ☐ Yes ☐ No

Have you tied your display ads together with any continuing theme? ☐ Yes ☐ No

Do you request proofs prior to running display ads? ☐ Yes ☐ No

Do you review ads for proper placement and errors? ☐ Yes ☐ No

What could you do to make your future display advertising more effective? _____

_____

_____

Have you ever used television advertising? ☐ Yes ☐ No

If yes, are you still using television for advertising? ☐ Yes ☐ No

If no, do you feel you gave it a proper evaluation? ☐ Yes ☐ No

How did you evaluate your television ads? _____

_____

What television medium have you used (cable, UHF, VHF)? _____

Do you use a "talking head" approach? ☐ Yes ☐ No

Do your ads feature yourself or other family members? ☐ Yes ☐ No

If yes, why?_____

_____

Is there a real estate showcase type program in your area? ☐ Yes ☐ No

If yes, do you advertise on it? ☐ Yes ☐ No

If not, why not?_____

_____

Is there a cable television bulletin-board station in your area? ☐ Yes ☐ No

Have you ever used it? ☐ Yes ☐ No

If you use television commercials, is a storyboard prepared? ☐ Yes ☐ No

Who prepares it? _____

If you use television commercials, who films them? _____

Who directs them? _____

Are any features and views desired conveyed to the cameraperson? ☐ Yes ☐ No

Are you (or a representative) present at filming? ☐ Yes ☐ No

Do your television commercials feature testimonials? ☐ Yes ☐ No

Real-life situations? ☐ Yes ☐ No

Do you intend to use television in the future? ☐ Yes ☐ No

What can you do to increase the effectiveness of your television advertising dollars? _____

_____

_____

_____

Have you ever used radio as an advertising medium? ☐ Yes ☐ No   For institutional ad use? ☐ Yes ☐ No   For new developments? ☐ Yes ☐ No   For individual homes? ☐ Yes ☐ No   For listings? ☐ Yes ☐ No

How did you choose the station and time slots? _____

_____

Who prepared your radio advertising? _____

How did you evaluate the effectiveness of your ads? _____

_____

Do you intend to use radio in the future? ☐ Yes ☐ No

How could you increase radio ad effectiveness? _____

_____

How would you evaluate future responses to your ads? _____

_____

Do you regularly market large properties to buyers outside your geographical area?   ☐ Yes   ☐ No

Have you ever prepared a video to promote a property?   ☐ Yes   ☐ No

Would the use of videos significantly help your firm?   ☐ Yes   ☐ No   How? _____

_____

Do you know the cost of movie-screen advertising in your market area?   ☐ Yes   ☐ No

What benefits, if any, do you feel movie-screen advertising would provide for your firm? ____

_____

_____

Have you ever tested movie-screen advertising?   ☐ Yes   ☐ No

Do you or your staff use the telephone for soliciting buyers or sellers?   ☐ Yes   ☐ No

Do you use a reverse directory for solicitation?   ☐ Yes   ☐ No

Have you prepared scripts to aid in telephone presentations?   ☐ Yes   ☐ No

What could you do to increase the effectiveness of telephone solicitations? _____

_____

_____

Do you market any large developments?   ☐ Yes   ☐ No

Have you considered outdoor advertising (billboards and bulletins)?   ☐ Yes   ☐ No

Are you currently using outdoor advertising?   ☐ Yes   ☐ No

How have you evaluated the effectiveness of outdoor advertising? _____

_____

What can you do to increase the effectiveness of your outdoor advertising? _____

_____

_____

Is bus-shelter advertising available in your market area?   ☐ Yes   ☐ No

Do you have listings that could be effectively advertised on bus shelters?   ☐ Yes   ☐ No

If you had a painted van to promote your firm, how would you use it? _____

_____

_____

If you had a travel trailer, how would you use it?_____

_____

_____

Does your office have any cartop or trailer-mounted signs?   ☐ Yes   ☐ No

If they were available, how would you use them? _____

_____

Would truck ads fit in with your office marketing needs?   ☐ Yes   ☐ No

If yes, how would you utilize truck signs? _____

_____

Is there a public transit system in your market area?   ☐ Yes   ☐ No

If yes, how could you utilize this advertising medium? _____

_____

_____

Do you (or your salespeople) regularly visit stores or locations featuring public bulletin boards?   ☐ **Yes**   ☐ **No**

Do you currently use bulletin boards to promote specific properties?   ☐ Yes   ☐ No

Does your local airport have rental display cases available?   ☐ Yes   ☐ No

How could you utilize airport advertising to further your advertising goals? _____

_____

_____

Have you considered an information booth for community events, swap meets, etc.?
□ Yes   □ No

What do you think the cost of such a display booth would be? $_____

If you had such a booth, where and how would you use it? _____

_____

_____

Does your office or staff use direct-mail advertising?   □ Yes   □ No

If yes, who prepares the fliers? _____ How do you evaluate the effectiveness of the mailing

pieces? _____

_____

Do you use mailings for: Listings?   □ Yes   □ No   Buyers?   □ Yes   □ No   Open houses
and openings?   □ Yes   □ No

Do you use testimonials in your mailings?   □ Yes   □ No

What could you do to increase the effectiveness of your firm's mailings? _____

_____

_____

Do you have any listings on special interest property likely to appeal to readers of a special
interest magazine?   □ Yes   □ No

Are there any magazines directed toward your market area?   □ Yes   □ No

Who do these magazines appeal to? _____

Do you have any properties likely to appeal to readers of such magazines?   □ Yes   □ No

Are there any home magazines in your area?   □ Yes   □ No

Do you feel you can effectively use home magazines to market property?   □ Yes   □ No

Why? _____

_____

Are free weekly papers available that cover your market area?   □ Yes   □ No

How does your market area correspond to their distribution? _____

_____

Do you know the cost for classified and display ads in these papers?　☐ Yes　☐ No

Have you test-marketed properties using this medium?　☐ Yes　☐ No

If not, why not? _____

_____

Do you feel you can effectively utilize free weekly papers?　☐ Yes　☐ No

If yes, how? _____

_____

_____

Would either your market area or the type of property you are marketing be of special interest to a particular national origin group?　☐ Yes　☐ No

If yes, are there foreign language papers serving that group in your area? _____

_____

Does anyone in your office speak the language of the group?　☐ Yes　☐ No

Do you intend to recruit salespeople from this group?　☐ Yes　☐ No

How can you best utilize foreign language papers? _____

_____

Would any of the properties you are marketing be of special interest to citizens of another country?　☐ Yes　☐ No

If yes, why? _____

_____

If you advertised in a foreign country, do you feel it would help you as to:　Sales?　☐ Yes　☐ No
Listings?　☐ Yes　☐ No

Are you listed in the white pages of the local telephone book(s)?　☐ Yes　☐ No

What are the real estate categories listed in the yellow pages of your local telephone book(s)? _

_____

_____

_____

Which categories are applicable to your firm? _____

_____

_____

Is your firm listed in those categories?   □ Yes   □ No

How many new people has your firm hired in the past year? _____

Have you had any promotions of personnel?   □ Yes   □ No

Have any salespeople passed a sales or listing plateau (such as $1 million in sales in one month)?   □ Yes   □ No

Has your firm made any significant sales or listings such as well-known buyers, sellers, previous owners, historical property, large properties, etc.?   □ Yes   □ No

Have you opened or moved an office?   □ Yes   □ No

Has any employee of your firm been active in any newsworthy activity?   □ Yes   □ No

Were all of the above covered by press releases?   □ Yes   □ No

If not, why not? _____

_____

Do your salespeople actively farm geographic areas?   □ Yes   □ No

If yes, does your office have a newsletter?   □ Yes   □ No

If not, why not?_____

_____

If you use a newsletter, how could it be improved?_____

_____

_____

Do all of your salespeople have listing presentation books?   ☐ Yes   ☐ No

If not, why not?_____

_____

_____

Does your office supply the basic material for the "why list?" and "why our firm?" portions of the listing presentation book?   ☐ Yes   ☐ No

If not, why not?_____

_____

_____

How could your listing presentation material be improved? _____

_____

_____

Does your office prepare property briefs for all new listings as soon as the listings are taken?   ☐ Yes   ☐ No

If not, why not?_____

_____

Do your property briefs include a photograph or line drawing of the property?   ☐ Yes ☐ No

Does the picture reproduce well?   ☐ Yes   ☐ No

If not, what should you do? _____

_____

Do your salespeople canvass door-to-door?   ☐ Yes   ☐ No

If yes, do you use door hangers?   ☐ Yes   ☐ No

If not, why not? _____

_____

Does your office send out Christmas or holiday cards?   ☐ Yes   ☐ No

If yes, what is special about your cards? _____

_____

How could your office effectively use coupons or contests in marketing property? _____

_____

_____

_____

Do you market any subdivisions?   ☐ Yes   ☐ No

If yes, what media do you use? _____

_____

How have you promoted grand openings?_____

_____

_____

What type of handouts do you use?_____

_____

_____

How do you direct traffic to your subdivisions? _____

_____

_____

How could you improve your subdivision marketing? _____

_____

_____

_____

Do a great many of your buyers come from other areas?   ☐ Yes   ☐ No

If yes, could a visitation package including lodging be advantageous to your firm?
☐ Yes   ☐ No

If yes, what should be included in the package? _____

_____

_____

How would you market it? _____

_____

_____

How do you currently promote open houses? _____

_____

_____

Does your office supply: Directional signs? ☐ Yes ☐ No Open house magnetic car signs? ☐ Yes ☐ No Flags and banners? ☐ Yes ☐ No Mobile open house office? ☐ Yes ☐ No Open house lawn signs? ☐ Yes ☐ No

How could you improve your open house marketing? _____

_____

Have you conducted any open house for agents? ☐ Yes ☐ No

How did you promote the agent open house? _____

_____

What could you do to make agent open houses more effective? _____

_____

The following case studies are included to show practical examples of utilizing various media, and can be used to assist you in developing an advertising plan aimed at your particular needs.

★ CASE STUDY   Classic Realty

Ralph and Mary have just left Jones Realty to open their own office. They have leased a small office in a strip shopping area and have chosen the name Classic Realty. Designed with a Roman column, the firm's logo is conveyed throughout their office decor, office sign, For Sale signs, stationery and calling cards.

Because they had been active in selling lots and land to builders as well as marketing new homes for builders, they intend to specialize in this area. One of their former associates has come to work for them and she has just listed a 68-lot development where the builder will have two model homes completed in 60 days. The development is across the road from a large 800-lot development. The grand opening of this large development is in 25 days.

ADVERTISING PLAN

I. *The New Subdivision*
Of immediate concern is the need to plan the marketing of the new subdivision. They will have to consider the following:

A. Staff recruitment. They will need classified ads aimed at attracting salespeople who have been successful in new tract sales. They should also network with salespeople with whom they have worked before to obtain recommendations for contacts.

B. Pre-opening sales. To take advantage of the grand opening traffic generated by the major development, they should plan a simultaneous pre-grand opening even though their models are not ready. They will need the following:

1. A large travel trailer (preferably with two doors) or a rental construction trailer with the development's name, the Classic Realty name as agent and their logo painted in the firm's colors. In large letters, should be painted "pre-opening sales office."

2. Banners, flags on tall poles, directional signs and entry sign.

3. Handout material showing floor plans, exterior views, what is included and prices. This material can be photocopied on colored sheets (for each plan).

      4. Press releases with artist's renderings of models (these could be the same or those prepared for planning commission approval).

      5. A billboard at project entrance showing renderings of models as they will look when completed and landscaped. A pre-opening price should be shown on a strip on the sign.

      6. A pre-opening extra should be negotiated with the developer such as an extra included with the sale, or pre-opening price break. By pointing out to prospective buyers that their deposit will be refundable if they do not approve of the models (their deposit is being held in trust), it is possible to make sales at this point.

      7. With proper signs the pre-opening should not really require additional advertising. The competitor's grand opening will bring in traffic, which will then be attracted to your signs.

  C. Grand opening

      1. Coordinate dates with the developer to make certain models are finished, landscaped and furnished, and that parking areas are provided for grand opening.

      2. Order all signs including the following:

        a. grand opening signs and banners

        b. traffic directional signs

        c. model home identification signs

        d. feature signs for the models

      3. Prepare all handout materials for prospective buyers.

      4. Prepare display ads for grand opening. Check portfolios of freelance artists and copywriters to select one and explain features you want emphasized.

      5. Make decisions on what newspapers to use for advertising.

      6. Prepare press releases for grand opening.

      7. Consider radio and/or television advertising. If you decide to use either, begin working on ads and booking airtime.

      8. Consider using a special attraction such as a tethered hot-air balloon.

      9. Consider the fact that your competitor, by continuing advertising, will bring in traffic. Therefore, you will not need as much in print and electronic media ads as would otherwise be required.

II. *Listings on Land/Lots*

  A. Send direct-mail promotions to owners (get addresses from tax rolls) indicating that the letter will be followed up with a telephone call. Special effort should be made to contact owners living outside the geographical area.

    B. A listing presentation book should be prepared for landowners.

III. *Marketing Land/Lots*

    A. Send regular mailings to builders showing land/lots available including price and terms if applicable.

    B. Make telephone calls to builders as to their needs.

    C. Place classified ads.

IV. *Listings on Homes/Subdivision*

    A. Send letters to builders indicating you will be contacting them.

    B. Make calls to builders to set up appointments.

        1. Listing presentation book (or video—see Chapter 5). Any listing presentation book should be specifically aimed at builders and show your work for others, as well as testimonials from other builders.

        2. Sample property brief on one of the builder's properties.

V. *Additional Considerations*

Ralph and Mary should also be concerned with:

    A. Name tags for all employees.

    B. Car signs for all salespeople.

    C. The office display; this is a good place for color renderings of the development.

    D. Obtaining "talking" house broadcasting equipment. This approach is excellent for homes under construction and developments prior to opening. A two-minute message can give features of the property (machines might need battery power). Having these machines would also be a powerful builder listing tool.

★ CASE STUDY   Sunshine Realty

Helen, a recently retired broker, moved to Sunny Acres, a guard-gated, 900-space mobile home community with a golf course, primarily for retirees. The units, which are double-wides and triple-wides, resell from between $70,000 to well over $100,000. The development has many recreational activities and clubs, but Helen found herself bored after about six months. She also discovered there were other retired real estate professionals who would like to be active again, but don't like the hectic approach of general real estate brokerage.

    Helen decides to go back into business, aiming at the major market share. Her goal is to be the dominant broker in Sunny Acres. The development and management firm still has a

FIGURE 10.1   For Sale Sign Utilizing High-Contrast Lettering and Silhouette Identifier

resale office in the development although all lots have been sold. They handle about one-third of the resale business with the rest divided among many area real estate firms.

Helen leases a storefront location with good visibility and signage possibilities about a quarter-mile from the entrance to Sunny Acres. She chooses a name that would associate her firm with Sunny Acres but would not confuse people as to the Sunny Acres Development and Management Company, which had developed Sunny Acres: She decides on Sunshine Realty. Her logo is a bright sun with radiating rays. The sun embellishes her For Sale signs so the outline of the sign immediately tells viewers it is her firm. Helen chooses a dark blue background with yellow reverse lettering for maximum contrast (figure 10.1).

She carries the logo and colors into her folded cards, which also feature photos on the inside. She uses the same colors in her office signs as well. She also includes "the Sunny Acre resale specialists."

Helen hires four full-time sales associates from among her acquaintances. She also encourages several retirees with extensive sales backgrounds to take licensing courses.

To obtain immediate name identification in Sunny Acres, Helen paints her golf cart dark blue with her logo and name in yellow. She also pays to have her employees' golf carts painted. Helen does this not only to attract attention but also because she believes that showing homes by golf cart in a golf-related retirement community will appeal to potential residents and will also be fitting with the temperament of her staff.

Helen also has magnetic car signs made with her logo, name and telephone number, and also provides name tags for her staff.

Because buyers come from a wide area, Helen decides to limit her local classified ads to block ads indicating she has the inventory and price range for homes in Sunny Acres. Helen does take a full-page ad in each issue of a real estate showcase magazine available at broker offices and free display racks. It is also sent out by the chamber of commerce with their material when there are inquiries.

Because community activities get so much attention in a retirement community, Helen decides to sponsor a senior softball team. She also donates golf caps with her logo on them for prizes for local events. Because everyone is from the area, she feels she gets good exposure from the caps. Her salespeople also give out plastic sunshades to people they talk with, again with her firm logo.

Helen has an electronic bulletin board close to the street in front of her office which advertises a particular unit.

Helen's best advertising tool is the monthly *Sunny Acre Times*, a tabloid, four-page newspaper she prepares and distributes. The four pages are devoted entirely to Sunny Acres. It includes news items such as golf tournaments, photos, local activities, special events, illnesses, anniversaries, etc., as well as a free classified ad section for items under $1,000. The back page belongs to Helen: It is an advertising page devoted to photos of homes available through Sunshine Realty. Because of the important information the newspaper contains, it is sought by residents and often sent to friends who are interested in relocating. Helen receives many mail requests for copies.

To produce this paper, Helen has found a local resident who has had newspaper experience to be editor. She is supplied desk space, telephone, expenses and her name on the masthead as editor in chief. The effect of the paper along with other advertising has been to give Sunshine Realty the major market presence and dominate the new listings. Helen says, "The firm that controls the inventory controls the sales."

★ CASE STUDY   **TBS-Gordon Realty, Inc.**

TBS-Gordon Realty, Inc., is a franchise of a national real estate franchisor, TBS. Tom Kane was recently hired as general manager and broker for TBS-Gordon Realty, Inc., after Jerry Gordon, the President, suffered a stroke.

TBS-Gordon Realty, Inc., has been in business 29 years at the same location, the last eight years as a TBS affiliate. They are located in a large suburb of a major metropolitan area. The area has been undergoing transitional change. In the past five years the Mexican-American population grew from less than 1 percent of the population to 28 percent.

Over the last two years, the brokerage operations of TBS-Gordon Realty, Inc., has operated at a loss. The loss has been more than offset by the profit from the buying and selling activity of Jerry Gordon. In fact, Mr. Gordon has devoted most of his time to these activities.

Listings are the strongest element of their brokerage operation, as several of the agents have worked hard developing owner contracts. However, more than 80 percent of the firm's listings sales have been sold through other firms. As a result, office commissions have decreased. The office currently has 11 salespeople, but has employed as many as 20 salespeople.

TBS-Gordon Realty, Inc., pays a percentage of its gross toward corporate advertising. Direct advertising by TBS-Gordon Realty, Inc., consists of:

- A weekly one-half page block ad of their properties in the Sunday Classifieds of the major metropolitan paper covering the area (cost $1,600 per week).
- Small classified ads in the daily editions of the major metropolitan paper.
- Three daily 60-second radio spots on a station playing mostly golden oldies.

The following were institutional advertising:

- Sponsorship of a bowling team.
- Car signs, office signs, cards, for sale signs, etc., carrying a TBS logo.
- Window displays of available properties.
- Property briefs of all listings.

The area is also served by several other radio stations, one of which is a Spanish-language station, several television stations, a local weekly suburban paper, several "shopper" papers and a daily Spanish language newspaper. TBS-Gordon Realty, Inc., does not use any other advertising media. Of the 11 salespeople, only one speaks Spanish. Tom Kane had three years of high-school Spanish and some Spanish language skills, but is not fluent in the language.

Tom Kane decides changes are necessary if the firm is to survive. He feels it is necessary that TBS-Gordon Realty, Inc., develop a niche market supremacy. The Mexican-American market appears to be the growing niche market. Tom feels he has to reach this market and align the firm closely to the market. To accomplish this, he takes the following steps:

- He advertises in the Spanish language paper for a salesperson. The ads point out that licensing is required, but TBS-

Gordon Realty, Inc., will pay one-half the cost of licensing courses for those selected. Tom's decision to advertise for unlicensed persons is based on the fact that the local Board of Realtors has very few members with Spanish surnames.

- Tom sends registered letters to real estate salespersons having Spanish surnames, stating that he would like to meet with them and discuss a new program offering an exceptional opportunity. He uses registered letters to emphasize the importance of the letter.

- Tom purchases folding booths with large display surfaces. Each booth will display pictures of properties and information on the properties in both English and Spanish. The booths will be set up at area swap meets as well as religious and ethnic festivals.

- In order to create area goodwill, Tom decides to sponsor a local soccer team. He regards this as pure institutional advertising.

- Tom stops advertising in the major metropolitan paper as soon as he hires three Spanish-speaking employees.

- Tom has made ad writing a major project, devoting considerable time to fitting ads to various media. While he feels his advertising responses have improved, records had not been kept in the past as to calls on ads. Tom inaugurates a logging system for calls so he can judge effectiveness of ad appeals and the individual advertising media.

- Tom advertises a different property each day on the Spanish-language radio station with three one-minute commercials. He cancels the firm's other radio advertising.

- Tom places a large weekly block ad on properties available in the area's weekly paper.

- Tom places five to eight small ads on different properties in each of the two weekly "shopper" papers.

- Using the Spanish-langauge paper, Tom places a block ad in Spanish, showing a number of properties.

- Tom has encouraged a Spanish speaking salesperson to write a weekly real estate column for the Spanish language paper.

- Using corporate TBS material and the help of a graduate student in film-making, Tom Kane prepares a two-minute Spanish commercial extolling the virtues of TBS-Gordon Realty, Inc. This commercial is shown nightly at the three Spanish language movie theatres in the area.

- Open house signs are printed in Spanish.

- All property briefs include a Spanish translation.

- In addition to helping bring in buyers, sellers are not forgotten. The firm prepares listing material, homeowners mailings and a listing presentation book in both English and Spanish.

★ CASE STUDY   **Mountain Village Realty**

Mountain Village Realty is located in the resort town of Mountain Village. The town's economy is based on tourists, primarily skiers. Approximately 70 percent of the firm's sales are December through March. Approximately 20 percent are June through September with a few sales in fall and spring. The village is overflowing with people in winter and practically deserted in spring and fall, although over one-half of the facilities remain open. The hotels have between a 30 and 40 percent occupancy rate in summer with a number of weekends fully booked.

Mountain Village Realty is located in a picturesque shopping area of boutiques and restaurants. At least one-half of the sales result from the firm's very inviting window displays and attractive "Northwoods" interior decor complete with antiques and a large, round potbellied stove. Salespeople dress in ski clothes and boots. Besides being practical, the apparel fits in with the resort image. Everyone at the firm wears a name tag.

The sales records of Mountain Village Realty indicate that while visitors to the area come from a scattered geographical area, 60 percent of the buyers come from three metropolitan areas (in other states) within 700 miles of Mountain Village.

Mountain Village Realty's advertising consists of the following:

- Attractive window displays and signs.
- A welcoming interior decor.
- A one-half page ad in the weekly village paper including pictures of at least four of the properties.
- Distinctive For Sale signs.
- Individual calling cards complete with each salesperson's photograph.
- Property briefs (with pictures) for all listings. They are given to visitors, cooperating agents and mailed with responses to property inquiries.
- Open house flags, banners and large directional signs.
- Two distinctive office four-wheel drive vehicles, painted with the firm's sign colors and logo, which are used to show property in winter and during bad road conditions.
- Direct mailings from the tax roll for listings.

Mountain Village Realty has six full-time salespeople. Prices for listings range from $50,000 for a one-bedroom condominium to over $500,000 for a choice chalet. The salespeople all have an above-average income and there have been no staff changes in the past two years.

Broker Ralph Clifford, while happy with the firm's accomplishments, wants to increase spring and fall activity in particular as well as increase summer sales. To accomplish these goals Ralph has prepared and implemented the following plan:

- Ralph prepares a booth to be used at vacation and sports shows in the three major metropolitan areas from where the majority of his buyers are from. (These shows are generally held in the spring and fall.) The booth has large color photographs of available property as well as handout material.
- Ralph obtains an interstate "800" number, which is prominently printed on all the handout material.
- Ralph sets up a vacation package for visitors and includes a colored flier about the vacation package in all of his handout material. The vacation package consists of three days and two nights for two at one of the area's finest hotels, a free trip on a ski lift, discount tickets for meals, horseback riding, bicycle and car rentals, movies, retail merchandise, etc. The package is good on any day for the months April through June, and September through November (except holiday weekends). The package can also be used Sundays through Thursdays in July and August. The price of $84.50 covers all costs of the vacation package, and reservations that can be charged to a credit card are made by calling the "800" number at Mountain Village Realty. In this way, Mountain Village Realty knows who is coming and when.
- Ralph negotiates for the use of a large lobby display case showing available properties at the hotel he features in his vacation package.
- Letters to all property inquiries now include both the vacation package material and, of course, the "800" number.
- Using the "800" number, Ralph has begun placing classified ads under vacation property categories in metropolitan area newspapers where most of the buyers come from. Ralph is able to evaluate media effectiveness as well as specific ad appeal so he can plan the future use of classified ads. He sends vacation package information to all ad inquiries, which are followed up by salesperson's telephone calls.
- Ralph now features the firm's "800" number on all direct mailings for listings, as well as the firm's stationery and business cards.

★ CASE ANALYSIS   Your Firm

Your goal _____

_____

_____

_____

Anticipated office commission:

(Company dollar) based on implementation of your goal for the next 12 months: $ _____

Percentage of office commission to be allocated for advertising: $ _____

Your advertising budget for the coming year: $ _____

Your advertising plan:

Media _____

Use of media _____

_____

_____

Media _____

Use of media _____

_____

_____

_____

Media _____

Use of media _____

_____

_____

_____

Media _____

Use of media _____

_____

_____

Media _____

Use of media _____

_____

_____

Additional areas needing change: _____

_____

_____

_____

_____

_____

_____

_____

_____

_____

_____

Now assign a dollar allocation to the various media based on media cost and planned use.

$ _____

(Your total expenditures cannot exceed your budget.)

Index

Get the Performance Advantage
on the job. . .*in the classroom*

Order Number	Real Estate Principles and Exam Prep	Qty.	Price	Total Amount
1. 1510-01	Modern Real Estate Practice, 12th edition		$34.95	
2. 1510-02	Study Guide for Modern Real Estate Practice, 12th edition		$13.95	
3. 1961-01	Language of Real Estate, 3rd edition		$28.95	
4. 1610-07	Real Estate Math, 4th edition		$15.95	
5. 1512-10	Mastering Real Estate Mathematics, 5th edition		$25.95	
6. 1970-04	Questions & Answers To Help You Pass the Real Estate Exam, 4th edition		$21.95	
7. 1970-06	Real Estate Exam Guide: ASI, 3rd edition		$21.95	
8. 1970-09	Guide to Passing the PSI Real Estate Exam		$21.95	

Advanced Study/Specialty Areas

9. 1520-02	ADA Handbook: Employment and Construction Issues Affecting Your Business		$29.95	
10. 1560-08	Agency Relationships in Real Estate		$25.95	
11. 1978-03	Buyer Agency: Your Competitive Edge Real Estate		$25.95	
12. 1557-10	Essentials of Real Estate Finance, 6th edition		$38.95	
13. 1559-01	Essentials of Real Estate Investment, 4th edition		$38.95	
14. 1556-10	Fundamentals of Real Estate Appraisal, 5th edition		$38.95	
15. 1556-14	How to Use the Uniform Residential Appraisal Report		$24.95	
16. 1556-15	Introduction to Income Property Appraisal		$34.95	
17. 1556-11	Language of Real Estate Appraisal		$21.95	
18. 1557-15	Modern Residential Financing Methods, 2nd edition		$19.95	
19. 1556-12	Questions & Answers to Help You Pass the Real Estate Appraisal Exams		$26.95	
20. 1551-10	Property Management, 4th edition		$35.95	
21. 1560-01	Real Estate Law, 3rd edition		$38.95	
22. 1556-18	Uniform Standards of Professional Appraisal Practice		$19.95	

Sales & Marketing/Professional Development

23. 1913-04	Close for Success		$18.95	
24. 1907-06	How to Develop a Six-Figure Income in Real Estate		$22.95	
25. 1916-11	Finding & Buying Your Place in the Country		$24.95	
26. 1909-06	New Home Selling Strategies: A Handbook for Success		$24.95	
27. 1913-01	List for Success		$18.95	
28. 1922-06	Negotiating Commercial Real Estate Leases		$34.95	
29. 1913-11	Phone Power		$19.95	
30. 1907-05	Power Real Estate Advertising		$24.95	
31. 1926-03	Power Real Estate Letters		$29.95	
32. 1907-01	Power Real Estate Listing, 2nd edition		$18.95	
33. 1907-04	Power Real Estate Negotiation		$19.95	
34. 1907-02	Power Real Estate Selling, 2nd edition		$18.95	
35. 1965-01	Real Estate Brokerage: A Success Guide, 3rd edition		$35.95	
36. 1913-13	The Real Estate Sales Survival Kit.		$24.95	
37. 1978-02	Recruiting Revolution in Real Estate		$34.95	
38. 1903-31	Sold! The Professional's Guide to Real Estate Auctions		$32.95	
39. 2703-11	Time Out: Time Management Strategies for the Real Estate Professional		$19.95	
40. 1909-04	Winning in Commercial Real Estate Sales		$24.95	

NEW! Audio Tapes

41. 1926-06	Power Real Estate Listings		$19.95	
42. 1926-05	Power Real Estate Selling		$19.95	
43. 1926-04	Staying on Top in Real Estate		$14.95	

Book total	
Tax	
Shipping and Handling	
Less $1.00 off if you fax order	
Total amount	
	R92005

Shipping/Handling Charges:

$0-24.99	$4
$25-49.99	$5
$50-99.99	$6
$100-249.99	$8

Order shipped to the following states must include applicable sales tax:

CA, FL, IL & NY

Real Estate Education Company
Where Experts Begin

a division of Dearborn Financial Publishing, Inc.

520 North Dearborn Street, Chicago, IL 60610-4354

Place your order today! **By FAX: 1-312-836-1021.** Or call **1-800-437-9002, ext. 650**
In Illinois, call 1-312-836-4400, ext. 650. Mention code R92005. Or fill out and mail this order form to:
Real Estate Education Company, 520 North Dearborn Street, Chicago, Illinois 60610-4354

Your Satisfaction is Guaranteed!

All books come with a 30 day money-back guarantee. If you are not completely satisfied, simply return your books in saleable condition and your money will be refunded in full.

☐ Please send me the Real Estate Education Company catalog featuring your full list of titles.
Prices are subject to change without notice.

Fill out form and mail today!
Or Save $1.00 when you order by Fax: 312-836-1021.

Name _____

Address _____

City/State/Zip _____ ____

Telephone _____

Payment must accompany all orders (check one):

☐ Check or money order (payable to Dearborn Financial Publishing, Inc.)
520 North Dearborn Street, Chicago, Illinois 60610-4354

☐ Charge to my credit card: ☐ VISA   ☐ MasterCard

Account No. _____ Exp. Date _____

Signature _____
(All charge orders must be signed.)

2/93

Return Address:

_____

_____

‖‖‖‖

BUSINESS REPLY MAIL
FIRST CLASS   PERMIT NO. 88176   CHICAGO, IL

POSTAGE WILL BE PAID BY ADDRESSEE:

**Real Estate
Education Company**
a division of Dearborn Financial Publishing, Inc.

Order Department
520 North Dearborn Street
Chicago, Illinois 60610-9857

IMPORTANT • PLEASE FOLD OVER • PLEASE TAPE BEFORE MAILING

NOTE: This page, when folded over and taped, becomes a postage-free envelope, which has been approved by the United States Postal Service. It is provided for your convenience.

IMPORTANT • PLEASE FOLD OVER • PLEASE TAPE BEFORE MAILING